LOVING PSYCHOANALYSIS

LOVING PSYCHOANALYSIS

Technique and Theory in the Therapeutic Relationship

SUSAN S. LEVINE

JASON ARONSON
Lanham • Boulder • New York • Toronto • Plymouth, UK

Published in the United States of America
by Jason Aronson
An imprint of Rowman & Littlefield Publishers, Inc.

A wholly owned subsidiary of
The Rowman & Littlefield Publishing Group, Inc.
4501 Forbes Boulevard, Suite 200, Lanham, Maryland 20706
www.rowmanlittlefield.com

Estover Road
Plymouth PL6 7PY
United Kingdom

British Library Cataloguing in Publication Information Available

Library of Congress Cataloging-in-Publication Data

Levine, Susan S.
Loving psychoanalysis : technique and theory in the therapeutic relationship / Susan S. Levine.
p. cm.
Includes bibliographical references.
ISBN-13: 978-0-7657-0624-9 (cloth : alk. paper)
ISBN-10: 0-7657-0624-5 (cloth : alk. paper)
ISBN-13: 978-0-7657-0626-3 (electronic)
ISBN-10: 0-7657-0626-1 (electronic)
1. Psychoanalysis. 2. Psychotherapy. 3. Therapist and patient. 4. Empathy. 5. Caring. I. Title.
BF175.L486 2009
616.89'17—dc22 2008035556

Printed in the United States of America

∞™ The paper used in this publication meets the minimum requirements of American National Standard for Information Sciences—Permanence of Paper for Printed Library Materials, ANSI/NISO Z39.48-1992.

CONTENTS

Acknowledgments

I WOULD LIKE TO EXPRESS GRATITUDE TO THE MANY MENTORS, colleagues, students, supervisors, and supervisees who taught me and stimulated my thinking. It is especially humbling to write about unfamiliar disciplines, and I am deeply grateful to those who generously tried to educate me about their area of expertise. Some assisted me in finding relevant scholarly material; some read my work to ascertain that I was not making fundamental errors in my applications of alien and tantalizing ideas.

For their readings, critiques, encouragement, and/or other forms of support, I thank: Salman Akhtar, M.D.; Christine Anzieu-Premmereur, M.D.; Michele Berlinerblau, M.D.; Charles Brice, Ph.D.; Allison Chabot, Ph.D.; Stanley Coen, M.D.; Heather Craige, M.S.W.; Amy Demorest, Ph.D.; Denise Dorsey, M.D.; Ted Fallon, M.D.; Glen Gabbard, M.D.; Erik Gann, M.D.; the late Peter Giovacchini, M.D.; Jerry Gollub, Ph.D.; Michael Goodman, M.D.; Barbara Gray, Ph.D.; Axel Hoffer, M.D.; Theodore Jacobs, M.D.; Abigail Kay, M.D.; Stephen Kerzner, M.D.; Madeleine Levine, B.A., M.B.D.; Steven Levy, M.D.; Patrick Mahony, Ph.D.; Kenneth Newman, M.D.; William O'Brien, M.D.; Joanne Payson, M.A.; Warren Procci, M.D.; the late David Raphling, M.D., Owen Renik, M.D., Arnold Richards, M.D.; Arnold Rothstein, M.D.; David Scharff, M.D.; Melvin Singer, M.D.; William Singletary, M.D.; Barbara Shapiro, M.D.; Anne Sclufer, Ph.D.; Paul Shipkin, M.D.; Daniel B. Szyld, Ph.D.; and Carol Tosone, Ph.D.

In addition, I would like to recognize five others. Without the suggestions, patience, encouragement, and gentle nudging of Jason Aronson, M.D., over many years, I never would have dared to write. Sydney Pulver,

M.D., generously reads the first draft of everything I write; his enthusiasm, encouragement, and frankness are indispensable. My husband, Steven Levine, Ph.D.—one of the smartest and most learned people I know—is the reader to whom I turn with texts as they near a final version; his critiques are invaluable. Harry Smith, M.D., the unexcelled, patient, and rigorous editor of the *Psychoanalytic Quarterly*, challenged me intellectually and made significant contributions to the chapters originally published in that journal. Finally, I would like to express my profound gratitude to Alex Burland, M.D., who knew what he had contributed to my life and writing; this book is dedicated to his memory.

Last, but most, I thank my patients, who have allowed me to learn with them.

★ ★ ★

The author expresses her thanks to the George Bernard Shaw estate for generous permission to quote dialogue from the film *Pygmalion*.

She also gratefully acknowledges permission from the following journals to use material previously published in their pages:

—*The Journal of the American Psychoanalytic Association*, which published an earlier version of chapter 5 ("Nothing But the Truth: Self-disclosure, Self-revelation, and the Persona of the Analyst," *Journal of the American Psychoanalytic Association, 55*, 1, 2007).

—*The Psychoanalytic Quarterly*, which published earlier versions of chapters 2, 3, and 4 ("Beauty Treatment: the Aesthetics of the Psychoanalytic Process," *Psychoanalytic Quarterly, 72*, 4, 2003; "To Have and to Hold: On the Experience of Having an Other," *Psychoanalytic Quarterly, 73*, 4, 2003; and "Catching the Wrong Leopard: Courage and Masochism in the Psychoanalytic Situation," *Psychoanalytic Quarterly, 75*, 2, 2006).

—*The International Journal of Applied Psychoanalytic Studies*, which published an earlier version of chapter 1 ("On the Mirror Stage with Henry and Eliza, or Play-ing with *Pygmalion* in Five Acts," *The Journal of Applied Psychoanalytic Studies, 3*, 2, April 2001).

Introduction

I BEGAN MY CLINICAL CAREER FASCINATED by psychoanalytic theory. I wrote my first book in order to teach myself and help others learn what confused me about the variety of theories and why they were thought to be incompatible. From my then–vantage point outside psychoanalysis proper, it certainly seemed as though clinicians seemed to choose a single school. Perhaps this was less the case than I imagined. The thesis of that book was that one did not need to choose one theory over another; theories are "useful servants," available to serve us as we see fit. That book addressed the question of the fit between patient, analyst or therapist, and theory. This one, in a loose sense, addresses the fit, or match, between analyst and analysand. I have moved in the direction of exploring the analyst's experience as well as the patient's, and especially the pressures and desires—and pleasures—inevitable in doing the work of doing psychoanalysis and intensive psychoanalytic psychotherapy. I have come to believe that the proper working attitude of the analyst is not one of neutrality but of loving. This love should expressed through the deepest empathy of which the analyst is capable, through the disciplined use of the art and craft of attention and interpretation, thoughtful abstinence, considered anonymity, and the inevitable self-revelation and occasional self-disclosures each particular patient requires.

As I wrote each of these chapters, I gradually began to discover what I actually thought as a practicing analyst. Each essay functioned in a sense as a dream, something I produced that required interpretation and reflection. I became increasingly aware that I used theory in what sometimes felt to me to be a promiscuous manner. Why could I move so comfortably between theories that are generally thought to be incompatible? Why did I not feel drawn to be faithful to one theory or school? If pushed, I would have to declare more allegiance to the romantic vision than to the classic and to object relations and relational rather than drive theories; however, I would not wish to try to persuade anyone that any single view approaches anything like absolute correctness. People are neither uncivilized apes requiring determined interpretation and management of their base instincts nor flowers with closed blooms that simply await an analytic sunshine and watering in order to open—they are both. Psychoanalysis is about both/and—not either/or. I might say, perhaps, that I see psychoanalytic work as embedded within an intersubjective matrix, within which many varieties of theory may be useful. In the final chapter I attempt to offer a sketch of a theory of everything, a grand unifying theory of psychoanalysis, in order to reconcile my own theoretical eclecticism. Other writers have addressed the potential of chaos theory in useful ways; I summarize the ways in which I find this new science clinically helpful, and I then apply it as an approach to metapsychology.

Even as I make a move toward considering psychoanalysis to be, in the end, a science rather than an entirely hermeneutic discipline (or, rather, I envision a way to understand that hermeneutic activity as possessing a scientific character), I continue to believe that there will always seem to be an emergent or synergistic quality to psychoanalysis, a way in which it will and should always seem like alchemy rather than chemistry. We have come to understand a great deal of what makes a baby come into existence. We understand much of the science of the process, the genetics, and so forth. And yet the birth of a child nonetheless seems like a miracle, like magic. There remains a synergistic quality that, I do not believe, will ever be superseded by our knowledge of facts, processes, and mechanics. Likewise with psychoanalysis. No matter how much we may be able to understand the logically accessible, scientific elements in this work, there will always, I believe, remain a large element of art and perhaps alchemy—that, in some cases, psychoanalysis can turn coal into gold, or shit into platinum and diamonds.

In my chapter on the story of Henry Higgins and Eliza Doolittle, I use the Pygmalion myth and its modern incarnation as a parable for the psychoanalytic situation and the creativity that underlies and animates its every aspect. I explore both the joyful and the conflictual elements in creativity for both analyst and analysand, focusing on the potential coercive elements as well as on the loss involved in relinquishing any homeostatic constellation—even in order to attain a more satisfying or ostensibly higher level of functioning. This is the first of my three comments on the question of the match in which I explore, in the story's parable, the ways in which analysts and patients choose each other.

It is difficult to imagine that any patient seeking analysis does not have, on some level, in some form, a fantasy, wishful or fearful, of being made or remade by her analyst. In this chapter I address the power, if unconscious, in the analysand's choice of analyst as well as what I believe to be a common fantasy of creation held by analysts. Creation, from the patient's perspective, suggests birth or perhaps rebirth, since psychoanalysis does not work with tabula rasa patients, but with complexly formed individuals. From the perspective of the analyst, the activity of creation brings to mind artistic effort as well as parenthood, childbirth, and fertilization. This is a mode of activity and power in contrast to the experience of being created, a passive and (at least consciously) powerless position. I use in this chapter one of our modern versions of the ancient myth of Pygmalion—that of Henry Higgins and Eliza Doolittle. The myth of Pygmalion and Galatea, his fair lady, has received little attention in the psychoanalytic literature, perhaps because the sadism of Henry Higgins has overshadowed the benevolent side to his fantasy and actions. The Pygmalion character, in fact, can be understood to reside psychologically in between Narcissus and Oedipus. I offer the Pygmalion story as a powerful and cautionary parable for psychoanalysts—it is vital that we be aware of our desires to create and their inherent dangers.

Creative aggression in the analyst and the patient's wish to be changed become the red thread leading into the next chapter. I explore here the ways in which psychoanalytic creativity and growth for both analyst and analysand inevitably involve both courage and masochism. This chapter introduces the subject of courage into the psychoanalytic discourse about masochism and also demonstrates that ordinary ethical and axiological concerns can and should be included in our psychoanalytic language and practice. At each stage of an analysis, it may be helpful to consider whether the patient believes that taking a step deeper into the analytic relationship is both courageous and masochistic. This can open the door to exploration of conscious beliefs and how they are related to unconscious fantasies and assumptions. Considering the possibility that even a sadomasochistic enactment may simultaneously represent a courageous attempt to rework conflict or trauma can enrich the way we listen to both manifest and latent material. The title and illustrative metaphor come from the 1939 film, *Bringing Up Baby*, which involves the loss and recapture of Baby, a tame leopard. In true Hollywood madcap mode, Katherine Hepburn mistakes a dangerous circus leopard for Baby. Full of distress, hope, the wish to be changed, and the wish to remain the same, patients may have little awareness of the leopards they are dragging when they first seek help from us. Do we not help our patients confront, cage, and tame the unruly things they discover? I am repeatedly impressed by the way in which almost every patient entering psychoanalysis and psychotherapy experiences a similar predicament; and by how the issue reemerges at points when new areas of pain or conflict become apparent. And the courage-masochism experience is taking place not solely in our patients. Unlike the hapless Cary Grant, who was swept into Katherine Hepburn's sphere, we analysts know full well that we are going to be encountering untamed leopards of one sort or another. If analysis works, patients and analysts will always be getting into more than they originally bargained for. The psychoanalytic situation inevitably must evoke both courage and masochism in us as well.

In my chapter on self-disclosure and self-revelation, I continue exploring the role of the analyst. I focus here on what sort of honesty the analytic relationship requires. How do we reconcile the ethical need to be absolutely honest with patients with the equally important need not to reveal or disclose everything a patient withes to know about us? We analysts work in such conditions of anonymity that there is a pressure we all feel to be known for who we really are. The construct of the analytic persona may help organize how we make distinctions about which disclosures and revelations are appropriate and useful, especially in the face of interpersonal and relational theories that promote the use of these techniques. I propose that psychoanalytic honesty is not an all-or-nothing thing—that there are different levels of communication, and that one can withhold all or part of the "truth" while simultaneously remaining honest in one's communications. The persona of the analyst is a part or potential part of the analyst that is disclosed or revealed to the patient; it does not have to represent the entire truth of the analyst's being, although it must represent something that the analyst is able to assume, if only in fantasy, as part of his or her self. I believe that many analysts already have an unarticulated working concept of the analytic persona that describes the self we step out of at the close of each session; this working concept also guides us as we determine appropriate boundaries. Psychoanalysts have long known that patients perceive us in a manner that is determined by their own character and neuroses. What has been focused on much less is the way in which the analyst—with honesty, integrity, and in a style consistent with his or her own character and neuroses—appropriately structures and manipulates the data about him- or herself to which the patient has access.

In the final three chapters, I explore aspects of psychoanalysis that contribute to its *je ne sais quoi*—the unknown magical center, the sine qua non, the unnamable. In "Beauty Treatment," I expand on the theme of my awe and respect for the psychoanalytic process. I have come to think of psychoanalysis as a thing of beauty, approaching magic or alchemy in the way it can result in growth and transformation from a simple combination of two people talking in a room. What these people need to do is follow a set of guidelines for their conversations, with one of the two being responsible for both maintaining the integrity of those rules and determining when the rules would best be ignored or observed in a flexible and creative manner. Psychoanalysts enjoy doing analysis above and beyond its usefulness to patients; one reason for this lies in the aesthetic pleasure the analyst may derive from the analytic process. I discuss this aesthetic pleasure from the standpoint of meaning-making, communication, love, and professional craft. Patients may themselves seek in analysis a certain kind of beauty that is normally a byproduct of good enough empathy and communication. Using Kleinian theory, I examine the ways in which destructiveness and aggression may be understood in relationship to an aesthetic of psychoanalysis. I further propose that the aesthetic and ethical principles of psychoanalysis are indissolubly linked.

In "To Have and to Hold," I reconsider familiar concepts (such as internalization, object representation, and object constancy) in light of the notion of having in order to facilitate creative thinking about how patients are or are not capable of experiencing analysts—and how analysts allow them to do so. The meaning of Other-having is examined from both a theoretical and a subjective point of view. I suggest that the sense of having an Other results from positive real experiences, and that the ability to have an Other is the sine qua non, the building block, of all mental functions that require empathy. We do not know exactly why good parenting works, although we have some good guesses. We do not know exactly why bad parenting is disastrous, although, again, we have some good guesses. Our guesses are most accurate, I think, at the extremes. It seems pretty clear that the match between parents and child is central to the working or not working of the process; likewise, it is also pretty clear that the match between analyst and patient is crucial.

As I described above, in my final chapter on chaos theory and the fractal structure of psychoanalysis, I propose a unified view of both clinical phenomena and theoretical schools in psychoanalysis. My point of departure is the aesthetic element in the psychoanalytic relationship, which I described earlier. I suggest in my conclusion that this aesthetic may also reflect a deeper scientific and mathematic quality. I place the psychoanalytic relationship in the context of pattern-seeking and pattern formation that are ubiquitous in nature. Touching on the theories of Gödel and Heisenberg, I question the current pressure within the psychoanalytic field to present our field as equivalent to the "hard" sciences. My argument is that we do not need numbers, even though they might well be there underlying everything we do. Mathematicians and scientists, though, find beauty in their discoveries—and it is my hope that this book will encourage psychoanalysts and psychotherapists to rediscover the beauty and essential loving nature of our profession.

On the Mirror Stage with Henry and Eliza 1

Or, Play-ing with Pygmalion in Five Acts

Cast of Characters

Eliza Doolittle
Henry Higgins
Colonel Pickering
Mrs. Pearce
Alfred Doolittle
Mrs. Higgins
Freddy
Sigmund Freud
D. W. Winnicott
Heinz Kohut
Jacques Lacan

Produced and Directed by

Susan S. Levine

Act I—Playbill

It is difficult to imagine that any patient seeking analysis does not have, on some level, in some form, a fantasy, wishful or fearful, of being made or remade by her analyst.[1] Analysts have been advised to cultivate the "positive discipline of eschewing memory or desire" (Bion 1983, 31) in each clinical hour. If we have a "rule" must this not indicate that there exists a corresponding desire that must be suppressed out of the analytic ego? As Gabbard (1996, 41) writes: "Patients typically enter analysis with a conscious (or unconscious) fantasy that the unconditional love of the analyst will repair the damage done by the imperfect parents of their childhood. Similarly, a common unconscious determinant of the career choice of psychoanalysis is the hope that providing love for patients will result in the analyst being idealized and loved in return." It is with thoughts like this in mind that I contemplate the 1938 film, *Pygmalion*, a striking cautionary parable of psychoanalysis, noting with a certain dramatic irony that the span between this production and the original play of 1912 closely parallels the psychoanalytic career of Sigmund Freud.[2]

Many of the ways in which analysts commonly speak about psychoanalysis may be construed as partaking of a larger fantasy, or myth, of creation. Creation, from the patient's perspective, suggests birth, or perhaps rebirth, since psychoanalysis does not work with tabula rasa patients, but with complexly formed individuals. From the perspective of the analyst, the activity of creation brings to mind artistic effort as well as parenthood, childbirth, and fertilization. This is a mode of activity and power in contrast to the experience of being created, a passive and (at least consciously) powerless position. The fetus grows of its own power but without volition or awareness. Recall, too, that the gestational process, the mother's ultimate creative act, occurs without her conscious efforts. There is a lesson here for psychoanalysts, for as Casement (1990, 343) has pointed out, "therapeutic experience in analysis is found by the patient—it is not provided." Nevertheless, I believe that both doing psychoanalysis and being in psychoanalysis are profoundly creative activities, whether actively or passively so. The patient's desire to change—to feel better, to suffer less, to be different—and the analyst's desire to analyze—e.g., communicate understanding of, or influence the patient's thought processes, mental structure, and affective states—can be understood as part of a wish to create or be created. We also often talk about the patient's wish to change, influence, or affect the analyst. Less often do we mention that the analyst also may wish for the patient to change him—teach him how to be an analyst or a better analyst, broaden his horizons, or even repair him. Each of these elements exists both in fantasy and in the real relationship. And creativity involves, let us not forget, both loving and aggressive components. In the practice of psychoanalysis we must be acutely aware of the risks of enacting either participant's desire to create or be created. Such desires and gratifications may be part of the unobjectionable positive transference or countertransference and may thus elude recognition.

Despite some attention to the story of Pygmalion, one of the most compelling and provocative myths of creation, it has not entered the psychoanalytic lexicon in the ubiquitous manner of Oedipus and Narcissus. Perhaps the very power and popularity of Shaw's rendition of the myth explains why Pygmalion has not become part of the psychoanalytic discourse. The sadism and violence of Henry Higgins have overridden, it seems, any memory of the more benevolent aspects of the myth. The Narcissus myth, on the other hand, has found no such singular modern rendition. In contrast to this paucity of interest within our field, *The Oxford Guide to Classical Mythology in the Arts, 1300–1900s* lists some 191 different artistic treatments of the subject of Pygmalion from 1300 to the present (in comparison to 228 of the subject of Oedipus and 306 of the subject of Narcissus) (Reid 1993, 692–702, 754–62, 955–62). One particularly charming rendering of the Pygmalion story is not included in this list—Frankie Avalon's song, "Venus."

To take up the specifically Shavian twist to the story, our culture has an abiding fascination with impostors as well as with transformations. To name only a few examples, think of the films *Vertigo*, *Some Like It Hot*, *Being There*, *Tootsie*, *Pretty Woman*, *Mrs. Doubtfire*, and finally of *Six Degrees of Separation*, in which the Henry Higgins theme is made explicit. Other "mythic" characters of transformation might include Pinocchio and Coppélia.

I believe the story of Pygmalion has enormous potential, both as an elaboration of our understanding of narcissism in development, and, more immediately, as a parable for the psychoanalytic process itself. Giovacchini (1957) studied Shaw's style of communication in *Major Barbara*, and demonstrates the author's intuitive understanding of the technique of interpretation in clinical analysis. He argues that it is Shaw's wit and humor that contribute to the palatability of his socially subversive message: "Shaw in changing content was able to bring something to the surface that is in resonance with the audience's unconscious, and what he writes, thought it may be disputed at a reality level, has validity when considered in terms of psychoanalytic operations" (1957, 5). I believe Giovacchini's remarks apply to *Pygmalion* as well. Could it be that this was and is one of the blind spots in psychoanalytic thinking, that analytic thinkers who were clearly familiar with the Pygmalion myth did not want to see its relevance to the psychoanalytic situation? Are we uncomfortable about having wishes to create or recreate our patients? As Abend (1979, 595) cautions, it behooves the analyst to be aware of his own as well as the patient's fantasies of how psychoanalysis cures. Perhaps we should add the Pygmalion myth to our lexicon of fantasies of cure and wonder whether it may be a ubiquitous, even if not always predominant, component of the psychoanalytic encounter.

Act II—Sexuality and Fantasy, or What Kind of Love Is This?

Although we think of *Pygmalion* (and *My Fair Lady*) as a romance between Eliza Doolittle and Henry Higgins, let us remind ourselves that originally Eliza and Henry did not end up together. In the play itself, which Shaw subtitled, "A Romance in Five Acts," Eliza runs off to marry Freddy. In his rather extensive postscript to the play Shaw writes about why Eliza cannot marry Henry. First, Eliza is young and attractive enough that she is not forced to marry anyone simply to have a roof over her head. Second, Eliza was "instinctively aware that she could never obtain a complete grip of him, or come between him and his mother (the first necessity of the married woman)" (Shaw 1941, 136). Third, Eliza is not a masochist in Shaw's eyes: he writes that she "has no use for the romantic tradition that all women love to be mastered, if not actually bullied and beaten" (137). She will prefer to be the powerful one in the relationship, that is, with the hapless but devoted Freddy. And finally (148), "Galatea never does quite like Pygmalion: his relation to her is too godlike to be altogether agreeable." Following Shaw's explanation, we could see Henry not so much as a romantic figure but as a hero who uses his skills to rescue a member of the social and economic underclass. As Vesonder (1977, 42) points out: "Even a superficial examination of *Pygmalion* will show that the main focus of the play is not erotic involvement but the power of language and that Henry Higgins is more the hero than the lover."

It seems almost certain that there is a great deal of Shaw's autobiographical material in the character of Henry Higgins, particularly in regard to the relationship with the mother (Weissman 1958; Silvio 1995). Henry's denial of sexual and affectionate feelings for Eliza, his barely concealed aggression toward her as he teaches her, his ambivalent attachment to his mother, and his scorn for the social order of things hardly bespeak a soul absent of profound conflict. For Pygmalion, the creation of the statue is an attempt at sublimation, an attempt both to avoid a desired relationship with an object as well as to satisfy it, a developmental conflict that characterizes adolescence (Duez 1996). Richardson coined the phrase "the Pygmalion reaction" to refer to "the attempt to convert love into a less powerful emotion by giving it a rarefied and overesthetic quality" (1956, 458).

Psychoanalysts may perhaps breathe a sigh of relief at Shaw's original ending to the story in which the boundary between teacher and student, psychoanalyst and analysand, has not been violated. Yet even the actors who played on the stage were most unhappy with this ending (Weissman

1958; Vesonder 1977), and Shaw's 1938 screenplay ends with Eliza and Henry together, albeit ambiguously so. As Ovid, the Roman poet (43 BC–17 AD), tells it, however, the ending is quite clear: Pygmalion gets his woman (Ovid 1955). Shaw's refusal to match up Eliza and Henry in the play, though romantically unsatisfying, testifies to realistic doubts that a relationship begun in this fashion, rife with sadomasochism and empathic blind spots, could ever develop into a successful marriage. Writers have drawn convincing connections from elements in the plot of *Pygmalion* to Shaw's difficult childhood and resulting severe conflicts about relationships with women (Weissman 1958; Silvio 1995). As Weissman puts it:

> In the Galatean myth, Venus sanctions the womanhood of Galatea for its creator, Pygmalion. Shaw had no quarrel with the world in its pursuit of direct sexual gratification (giving the mistaken impression that it was true of him), but his major pursuit was a desexualized one. Throughout most of this life, his ego was master of the situation and he was able to desexualize and sublimate his erotic interests in women, which always had the outer form of a love affair (Weissman 1958, 551).

Pygmalion, the model for Henry Higgins, also expresses revulsion over a certain kind of female sexuality. As Ovid relates (1955, 241–43), Pygmalion lived in Amathus, on the island of Cyprus. He became disgusted by the women there who, refusing to "acknowledge Venus and her divinity," became the first prostitutes. Pygmalion thus elected to be celibate. But a yearning obviously remained, for he made an ivory statue, more beautiful than any living woman, and he fell in love with his creation:

> Pleas'd with his idol, he commends, admires,
> Adores; and last, the thing ador'd, desires.
> A very virgin in her face was seen,
> And had she mov'd, a living maid had been:
> One wou'd have thought she cou'd have stirr'd, but strove
>
> With modesty, and was asham'd to move.
> Art hid with art, so well perform'd the cheat,
> It caught the carver with his own deceit:
> He knows 'tis madness, yet he must adore,
> And still the more he knows it, loves the more:
> The flesh, or what so seems, he touches oft,
> Which feels so smooth, that he believes it soft.
> Fir'd with this thought, at once he strain'd the breast,

And on the lips a burning kiss impress'd.
'Tis true, the harden'd breast resists the gripe,
And the cold lips return a kiss unripe:
But when, retiring back, he look'd again,
To think it iv'ry, was a thought too mean:
So wou'd believe she kiss'd, and courting more,
Again embrac'd her naked body o'er;
And straining hard the statue, was afraid
His hands had made a dint, and hurt his maid:
Explor'd her limb by limb, and fear'd to find
So rude a gripe had left a livid mark behind:

. . . Pygmalion off'ring, first approach'd the shrine,
And then with pray'rs implor'd the Pow'rs divine:
Almighty Gods, if all we mortals want,
If all we can require, be yours to grant;
Make this fair statue mine, he wou'd have said,
But chang'd his words for shame; and only pray'd,
Give me the likeness of my iv'ry maid.

The golden Goddess, present at the pray'r,
Well knew he meant th' inanimated fair,
And gave the sign of granting his desire. (Ovid)

What is perhaps most striking to the modern—politically correct—reader is the exclusive focus on Pygmalion's desires and experience. Although the statue-come-alive came to be known as Galatea, in fact Ovid gives her no name in his text. He finishes his story by reporting that the two have a daughter, Paphos, for whom the island is named. It is ironic that Shaw, who was a dedicated feminist, in his effort to confer subjectivity on the "statue" has selected a female character who originally had no name. He might, after all, have called the play "Galatea." It appears that Shaw does not transcend his own sexual conflicts and his primary attachment, for in fact Eliza is named after his own mother.

Bergmann, in his scholarly treatment of the Narcissus myth (1984), elegantly argues that the Pygmalion story is another version of narcissistic love and that "Shaw should be credited with the insight that Pygmalion is a variant on the theme of Narcissus. The character of Professor Higgins is a composite of the two" (398). Bergmann points out that "[t]o Plato, all love was narcissistic and hermaphroditic, whereas to Freud, narcissistic love was only one type of love. . . . [N]arcissistic love is a love for a person other than the self, perceived subjectively as part of the self" (394). Bergmann goes on to suggest a link between a Pygmalion type of love (one which he categorizes as being a step beyond that of Narcissus, who was incapable of loving Echo) and the transitional object. Pygmalion, without doubt, fell in love with an Other, albeit one of his own creation. One of the most important features of the successful transitional object is that the parents allow it to exist, do not question its existence or the fact that the child has power over it (Winnicott 1971, 5–6). Could this be why Ovid gave the statue no name—that it is up to the child to name the transitional object and it is the parent's or author's job to play along? Winnicott also argues, of course, that cultural and artistic works are created within the transitional space (Winnicott 1971, 118). On a sexual level, Bergmann points out the progression from masturbatory love when the statue is but a statue to a narcissistic relationship when the statue comes to life; we might say here that the self has fallen in love with the self's object. Bergmann also hypothesizes hermaphroditic elements in this love, for "we may assume that Galatea represented the artist's own feminine aspects" (397). He suggests a link to fetishism, wittily pointing out Aphrodite's role as the therapist who has cured Pygmalion of this (398). Finally, Bergmann draws our attention to the fact that creativity in men may represent a sublimation of the envy of the capacity to bear children: "When this envy becomes too strong, the artist may wish that his art work could come to life, and when this wish is too strong, sublimation may be partly or entirely undone" (399). The statue was clearly Pygmalion's brainchild (a lovely—or perhaps I should say "loverly"—synonym for "idea").

Talpin, essentially supporting Bergmann's argument of this developmental progression in object relations, observes that the mirroring of the two mythic characters has distinguishing features. Narcissus uses water, a substance with little stability;[3] the image in the water is of only two dimensions, and the image is not something of his own creation. It is also an impermanent image, disappearing when he leaves the pond. Pygmalion, on the other hand, chooses a hard material (ivory); the object has the dimension of depth, and it is of his own creation. And it embodies a certain form of object constancy, continuing to exist even in the absence of the creator. Further, the Pygmalion tale involves procreation, which is not a part of the Narcissus story. Narcissus "lives in a world of impoverished drives"; his "object" is, in fact, himself. Pygmalion's relationship with the statue is a narcissistic one, but one that permits more expression of genital impulses even if with an object that was originally a selfobject (1997, 181–85). Duez (1996), too, uses the Pygmalion myth as an allegory of the development of object relations. From a predominantly Lacanian perspective, he stresses that every finding of an object is also a refinding, referring to the original loss of the mother at birth. Talpin emphasizes as well the separation inherent in Pygmalion's creating and then refinding of the object in contrast to the single undifferentiated act of Narcissus.

If psychoanalysts look to their own creator, they will discover a connection to the Pygmalion myth—an identification of psychoanalyst with sculptor. Freud makes only one reference to Pygmalion in his entire oeuvre (Guttman et al. 1980), and that is in the essay, "The 'uncanny.'" He comments that "we should hardly call it uncanny when Pygmalion's beautiful statue comes to life," supporting the thread of his argument that "[n]ot everything that fulfils this condition—not everything that recalls repressed desires and surmounted modes of thinking belonging to the prehistory of the individual—is on that account uncanny" (Freud 1919, 245–46). However, Freud became a Pygmalion of sorts when he wrote about a work of sculpture. Even though Freud originally published "The Moses of Michelangelo" in 1914 anonymously, Gay writes that "he cherished it almost as much as the statue it analyzes." He thought of this paper as a "love child" (1989, 314). As late as 1937 Freud spoke of the work of the analyst as molding clay, as he discussed the results of different types of analyses. He said, "we have an impression, not of having worked in clay, but having written on water" (1937, 241). Note here the same opposition between water and sculpture that we see as we compare the two myths. And in 1933 he described science as follows: "[I]t works as a rule like a sculptor at his clay model, who tirelessly alters his rough sketch, adds to it and takes away from it, till he has arrived at what he feels is a satisfactory degree of resemblance to the object he sees or imagines" (1933, 174). And one has only to look to the Dora case to see that Freud did in fact treat her in much the same way that Henry treated Eliza, with a peculiar mixture of respect and scorn, empathy and coldness, subjectivity and objectivity. (We must be sensitive, though, to the very different position women had in the first decade of this century. Freud's treatment of Dora may have represented at that time a rather extraordinary granting of the right of subjectivity to a young girl—after all, despite his problematic actions [see Mahony 1996] he believed her story and not her father's rendering of it.) In sum, I do not think it excessive to suggest that Freud had a rather strong identification with the role of Pygmalion.

Act III: Mirroring and Lack, or What Does Eliza Really Want?

Pygmalion opens as the theatre lets out on a rainy night in London. Theatre-going flora mix with common street fauna as people seek taxis or wait out the rain. Eliza tries to sell her flowers, has her first comical encounter with Freddy and his family, and then a bystander makes her aware that a man is taking down every word she is saying. It is at this moment that we see her first moment of intrapsychically based anxiety, and a telltale moment it is. Eliza blubbers her panic: "But I ain't done nothing wrong by speaking to the gentleman [Colonel Pickering, to whom she has tried to sell flowers]. I'm a good girl, I am. . . . [To Henry] What do you want to take down what I said for? You just show me what you wrote. How do I know you took me down right?" It is anxiety first about sexuality and then about mirroring. First, will the world take her to be a brazen and forward woman? Then will this strange man show her an image that she believes will represent herself accurately, that is to say, as she sees herself to be?

The sadomasochistic relationship is established here in the first conversation between Eliza and Henry as they begin the process of choosing each other as "patient" and "analyst." Their characters are exposed, and the central premise of the plot is laid down, as Henry displays what seems to Eliza to be a magical ability to know where she comes from. Through playful one-upmanship with his newly found friend, Colonel Pickering, Henry introduces the fantasy of "cure" that Eliza will attach to her own (conscious) dissatisfactions and (preconscious, one presumes) hopes and dreams.

> Henry: You see this creature with her curbside English, the English that will keep her in the gutter for the rest of her days. Well, sir, in three months, I could pass her off as a duchess at an ambassador's reception. . . . Or I could even get her a job as a lady's maid or as a shop assistant, which requires better English.
>
> Eliza: You mean, you could make me . . .
>
> Henry: Yes, you squashed cabbage leaf, you disgrace to the noble architecture of these columns, you incarnate insult to the English language, I could pass you off as the Queen of Sheba.

Henry fantasizes about Eliza at Covent Garden but chooses her at the moment when he accepts her fee; however, Eliza's moment of choosing Henry comes rather earlier. It is after she returns home in a taxi, paid for with Henry's loose change, that damp and fateful night. She returns to her room, lights the gas, fondly greets her pet bird, and settles down at what she must have hoped would pass for a vanity, flower basket on lap, to count the money. She then plays with her hair, lifting it as if to see what a different image of herself might look like. It is then that we see her mirror image, her face softens, and her eyes become full of possibility. Her preconscious idea has become conscious, and she has made her decision. Note that there are actual images of mirrors at other significant moments in the story as well—namely, the mirror in front of which Eliza cringes as she gets ready for her bath (Mrs. Pearce covers it to protect Eliza from the shame of seeing her naked body) and in the embassy ballroom the image in the mirror of the entering royalty, the ultimate societal mirror/judge of the results of the experiment. In a sense we could say that this entire script is about mirroring and about the relationship we have with the image we see of ourselves in different kinds of mirrors. It is also about how we choose the kind of image we present to others, how we manipulate the surface of the mirror.

When Eliza comes to see Henry to ask for English lessons, she says that she wants "to be a lady in a flower shop." This is her treatment goal, at least consciously. But it is the more grandiose goal in which Henry is interested—he and Colonel Pickering set out to "make a duchess of this draggle-tailed guttersnipe." Eliza calls him a bully, and says, "I never asked to go to Buckingham Palace, I didn't. If I knew what I was getting myself in here I wouldn't have come." Henry responds to her sputterings and doubts (which would seem to indicate her good reality testing, good judgment, as well as the capacity to sense narcissism in others) with a frank display of his power and of the difference between them; he plays for her the recording of her now famous lines: "I washed my face and hands before I came, I did." The image in the film here is of Henry, shot from a low angle, looking tall, powerful, and silent, seemingly letting the truth of her needy state and of his superiority be apparent. There is both courage and masochism (as I will describe in the next chapter) in Eliza's choice. Duez (1996, 125) refers to the understanding between the creator and the created, between Pygmalion and Galatea, as *un pacte narcissique* (narcissistic pact). The shared fiction is that the creator will not be affected by the object he has created, and that fiction is not shattered until after the reception when Henry is faced with the reality that the experiment has ended and that Eliza will be leaving.

Bernstein highlights the point that a patient may try to use analysis to remove a sense of being worthless and defective, to get "finished," to effect "a magical transformation" (1988, 229). One could speculate whether the fantasy of being finished plays into the termination phase of most analyses. It would seem likely that to a certain extent it is embedded in any patient's wish to be changed. For instance, a patient of mine fled treatment after the first intense transference/countertransference enactment that had been successfully put into words so that the patient could see the connections to her fantasies, her past, and her ways of relating outside the office. When she returned to treatment a few weeks later she expressed the poignant hope she had had that one day she would find a therapist who could say something that would make her all right, something that would wipe out her conviction that she had been irreparably damaged by her highly narcissistic and sadistic parents. She then proceeded to tell me a secret, one she had feared would so anger me that I would refuse to treat her any longer. Her doubt that she in fact deserved to feel better, her identification with the aggressor, prompted the attempted flight. The pressure of this terribly painful secret—as well as her continuing hope to be transformed—prompted the return.

Although Eliza must accept the bargain Henry and Pickering offer, in order for the colonel to foot the bill for the lessons, there are multiple suggestions of her strengths, feistiness, and capacity to tolerate Henry's ego-syntonic narcissism. She is downright playful with him as they bargain over the price, and she has thought carefully about what the lessons are worth, reasoning that he could not possibly charge as much as she knows one pays for French lessons from a real Frenchman—after all, this is her own language. He hesitates, at first, at her offer of a shilling an hour, but then accepts, explaining to Pickering that "a shilling to this girl is worth £60 or £70 to a millionaire. It's handsome, it's enormous, it's the biggest offer I've ever had." (Perhaps we have here a prototype of the low-fee analytic case!) Henry's empathic understanding of the true financial significance of her offer suggests that his narcissism is not total, that there exists a potential for change in him too. Poor Eliza, in a manner that seems inconsistent with the acute intelligence and symbolic capacity she demonstrates at the end of the film, is quite alarmed by this princely sum. Then again, the story really is a tale of magical transformation: When pronunciation and grammar are changed, so too is the capacity of the mind. Likewise in psychoanalysis, we work with the signifiers, with the external artifacts, and we effect a change in the patient's internal mental life. Indeed, it is signifiers that formed the very structure of the mind.

The fantasy underlying the treatment "contract" between Eliza and Henry would undoubtedly have been clearer to a turn of the century audience; "draggle-tailed" would have been understood to imply "sluttish" or "slatternly" (Meyer 1984). Hence, Eliza's famous protest, "I'm a good girl, I am." But it is certainly clear to us that Eliza seeks to be transformed from bad into good. It is when she sees her mirror image in her room that she finds herself wanting, and wanting something more. She locates this lack in her speech. But just as the phallus represents much more than the actual physical penis, speech represents power and possibility; it is a phallus-equivalent. As Meyer (1984, 238) points out, in *My Fair Lady* when Henry exclaims, "By George, I think she's got it!" we need not be confused about what Eliza's mastery of pronunciation means. Perhaps we could even say that she had had pronunciation envy! Graduation from Henry Higgins's "finishing school" (Bernstein 1988, 231), however, will be a Pyrrhic victory. Desire will remain unsatisfied, for it is always someone else who possesses the phallus. The subject has to recognize that there is desire, or lack in the place of the Other, that there is no ultimate certainty or truth, and that the status of the phallus is a fraud (this, for Lacan, is the meaning of castration). The phallus can only take up its place by indicating the precariousness of any identity assumed by the subject on the basis of its token (Rose 1985, 40).

For Eliza, learning to speak properly has been what Lacan would have called the pursuit of the *objet petit a*—that which represents the red herring of a desire that can never be truly satisfied. As Lee (1990, 144) puts it, it represents the "point of lack [where] the subject has to recognize himself." This is, for Eliza and all of us, a most painful process.

Act IV: Objectivity and Empathy, or Beyond the Looking Glass

Like Freud, Henry Higgins is most comfortable when he is not the one being observed; the first and last images of him in the film are of his back, his hatted head, and they are paired with frontal images of Eliza's face. Although she looks at him as he teaches her, like the good Freudian analyst he withholds himself: "The doctor should be opaque to his patients and, like a mirror, should show them nothing but what is shown to him" (Freud 1912, 118). While Henry shows Eliza a mirror image of what she shows to him, at least as the training starts, a fragmented, "bad," and objective image, it is Colonel Pickering who shows her an idealized mirror image, an image more whole than she feels. When he calls her "Miss Doolittle," or speaks to her in a gentle and courtly fashion, he gives her both a sense of empathic maternal interest and a sense of the possibility of gentlemanly recognition of her sexuality. As the training continues, Henry's frustration with Eliza's progress reflects her own experience that learning all this stuff is as difficult as talking with marbles in her mouth. But the crucial element in all this is that it takes place within the paradigm that mirroring is a necessary and desirable function.

Winnicott and Kohut have similar views on the developmental function of mirroring. In Winnicott's view, mirroring is closely related to creativity:

> A baby is held, and handled satisfactorily, and with this taken for granted is presented with an object in such a way that the baby's legitimate experience of omnipotence is not violated. The result can be that the baby is able to use the object, and to feel as if this object is a subjective object, created by the baby. . . .
>
> What does the baby see when he or she looks at the mother's face? I am suggesting that, ordinarily, what the baby sees is himself or herself. In other words the mother is looking at the baby and *what she looks like is related to what she sees there*. . . . If the mother's face is unresponsive, then a mirror is a thing to be looked at but not to be looked into (1971, 131–32; Winnicott's italics).

Kohut (1971) expanded the concept of mirroring in a systematic way to describe a variety of transference manifestations in the treatment of narcissistic difficulties. His definition is as follows:

> [T]he mirror transference is the therapeutic reinstatement of that normal phase of the development of the grandiose self in which the gleam in the mother's eye, which mirrors the child's exhibitionistic display, and other forms of maternal participation in and response to the child's narcissistic-exhibitionistic enjoyment confirm the child's self-esteem and, by a gradually increasing selectivity of these responses, begin to channel it into realistic directions (116).

Pygmalion, the play, was written at a most interesting time in the history of culture, for it was indeed when the act of looking and the value of the mirror had been put into question in a new way. For instance, Manet's *Olympia* (1863) puts the (male) viewer in the position of the client of the prostitute and his *Bar at the Folies Bergère* (1882) puts the viewer in the empty mirror in the position of painter/observer. The Cubists take issue with the ideal of mimesis—e.g., they question in a parallel way to Shaw whether the mirroring function is wholly desirable or accurate. And let us not forget the contribution of Freud, whose work told people that when they looked in the mirror, what they saw did not reflect more than a miniscule portion of their human complexity.

In our story, Henry begins with an exclusive—perhaps defensive—focus on the surface of the mirror, on the artifact of the paint on the canvas, while Pickering looks behind it to the perspective and depth of the image. The first hint that they will be playing with fire, that change cannot take place exclusively on the surface, comes when Pickering prods Henry to consider Eliza's subjectivity:

> Pickering: Doesn't it occur to you, Higgins, that the girl has some feeling?
>
> Henry: I don't think so. Have you, Eliza?
>
> Eliza: I've got my feelings, same as [h!]anyone else.
>
> Henry: You see the difficulty, Pickering.
>
> Pickering: What difficulty?
>
> Henry: To get her to talk grammar.
>
> Eliza: I don't want to talk grammar. I want to talk like a lady.

Eliza seems to be making a most Lacanian demand: "Fix the sound of my signifiers," she says. She appears to be colluding with Henry's focus on the surface. The treatment contract is based on a socially subversive, even perverse, alliance between Henry and Eliza, an agreement to challenge the social system in which language, pronunciation, is supposed to signal where one comes from. Henry wishes to rupture the relationship between signifier/signified and real world referent. Where Eliza wants to improve herself within the rules of the system, Henry wants to demonstrate that he is more powerful than the rules, more powerful than the name of the father (which Lacan locates in language itself, the medium of the symbolic order that interrupts the imaginary relationship between mother and infant).

But Henry does point out to Pickering that there is going to be a problem with the "signifieds." Even as he alludes to the problem of mind as opposed to the problem of pronunciation, he simultaneously appears to refuse acknowledging that mind includes emotions. Here, he and Eliza are in collusion, either unwilling or unable to foresee the inevitable and impossible position she will be in if she learns how to speak properly and can pass as a duchess. Should we say that this is a mis-alliance, a treatment plan based on a faulty premise? Unlike Lacan, whose analyst-as-master role was thin disguise for the aggressively asserted absence of *le sujet supposé savoir* (the subject who is supposed to know), Henry Higgins presents himself as the one who knows. And Eliza, who has her share of street smarts and may well know better, must accept Henry's image of himself as part of the bargain. His refusal to acknowledge what he sees suggests that a countertransference reaction is occurring, that he is like Freud, who knew what he wanted Dora to understand about herself. When Freud and Henry are excessively confident in their knowledge, they lose the capacity for empathy with Dora and Eliza. Indeed, Freud loses Dora and Shaw tried his best to have Henry lose Eliza.

Do all analyses work this way to a certain degree? It would be hard to imagine that any analyst would be better than good enough, would have no qualities that would impinge on the patient's needs. As Green points out, this is a dialectical relationship: "Inasmuch as the analyst strives to communicate with a patient in his language, the patient in return, if he wishes to be understood, can only reply in the language of the analyst" (1975, 3). But we should also remind ourselves of the necessity of optimal failure or optimal frustration in childrearing, teaching, and psychoanalysis. Does the patient sense during the selection process, consciously or not, the specific and idiosyncratic limitations of her future analyst? Is this, in fact, as significant a part of why she chooses this particular analyst as are his strengths, the optimism the initial contacts engender? For instance, an analyst caught up in the patient's material allowed an evaluation session to run over by about twenty minutes. On several occasions much later in the treatment, his enactment of his countertransference took the form of forgetting the times of this patient's appointments that had needed to be rescheduled or of ending a session early; the patient was not surprised. It would seem that just as the patient's material in the first session prefigures the treatment ahead, so too does the analyst's early stance foreshadow the likely pathway of the countertransference.

There is an interesting new literature developing on the impact the patient has on the analyst. We are all aware that there are patients with whom we do not wish to work and cannot work well. Correspondingly, there are patients we prefer, those we choose, although the active nature of our choice may be camouflaged by how we get referrals, by the seeming happenstance of how patients find us. Sometimes our colleagues who refer to us have made unconscious (or conscious) matches (Kantrowitz, 115). For example, colleague referred a woman to me for analysis. I had some strong countertransference reactions to the patient during her first few weeks on the couch, and as I studied what was happening I "discovered" how this patient's defensive style and manner of presentation bore a certain resemblance to my own. I found myself wondering how much of this my colleague had sensed. But no matter how patients come to us, when we take someone into treatment we have made a choice, conscious and unconscious. As Kantrowitz (1996, 215) points out: "Once the analytic process is underway, the reverberating nature of what transpires between patient and analyst often makes it difficult to tell where the process begins." This happens in long marriages as well, this effect of two mirrors held up to each other such that the source of the image is indeterminate. A colleague reported that several years into his analysis, he and his analyst greeted each other after the August hiatus to discover they had each grown a beard, not a word having been uttered by either person of his plan.

It is with shock that Henry Higgins realizes that Eliza has had an impact on him. He has come to depend on her; he misses her and is fond of her. Having denied the potential for Eliza to influence him, he is unprepared for his reactions. There are two interesting aspects to Henry's desire that Talpin (1997) points out in regard to the original *Pygmalion*. First, there is the wish to be both mother and lover—to be everything—to the newly alive statue—after all (ideally, at least), the mother is the first object the baby sees in this world.[4] Isn't it the case, Talpin asks, that from that point on it is Pygmalion's fantasy to be all for Galatea, to replace all other objects for her and to exclude all other objects from her? We can certainly see this in Henry's scorn for Freddy and disdain for his former pupil, Count Karpathy, when Eliza seems interested in them. Talpin's second point is that Pygmalion in fact passes from creator of the statue to receiver of its influence, and that there is a separation inherent in this. Henry does not want to separate from Eliza, and we can see this in his strenuous efforts to deny that he has moved from creator to receiver.[5] This movement from creator to receiver of influence is part of the normal passage parents must undergo as their child separates and individuates; the Pygmalion myth may be a valuable metaphor for this experience.

Henry's strenuous denial of his feelings brings to mind the earlier years of psychoanalysis when countertransference reactions were thought to indicate that there was something wrong, that one needed to return for further personal analysis. There were thus strong motives not to pay minute attention to countertransference, and certainly not to talk openly about it. It is no longer questioned that it is normal, expectable, and perhaps necessary for patients to affect their analysts profoundly, whether pleasurably or painfully. Glover's 1940 survey (cited in Kantrowitz, 207) reported that most analysts derived a therapeutic benefit from treating analytic patients, the "countertransference therapy." Sometimes, however, countertransference therapy turns into countertransference trauma when one's patients become uncannily aware of what one might not wish them to know.[6] Perhaps it is true that nothing of importance could ever happen in analysis without the kind of intentional vulnerability to the patient on the part of the analyst that make it possible for him to be influenced (Jacobs 1998). And perhaps the patient needs to know, consciously or unconsciously, that she has this power. Much of the time analysts do not share their experiences with the patient (Kantrowitz 1996); and there is ample reason not to disclose countertransference reactions on a routine basis. After all, part of the usefulness of the therapeutic relationship is in the patient's freedom to imagine her effect on the analyst—or in the exploration of why she feels she has no effect on him (see in this regard Aron 1991). It was certainly Eliza's experience that she had had little effect on Henry and even on Colonel Pickering, if one can judge by their behavior to her after the ball. She did not know consciously that she was no longer a squashed cabbage leaf to him, that she had gained the power to hurt him, not simply to displease him if she did not do well in her studies. But Eliza comes to learn that even the proud and self-sufficient Henry Higgins has made himself vulnerable to her from his place beyond the looking glass.

Act V: Self-analysis and Subjectivity, or The Statue Comes to Life

What is the crisis in *Pygmalion*? For Eliza, it is when she learns after the ball that mirroring is not sufficient. With painful clarity she has seen an image of herself as beautiful, as ideal, and it has not transformed her inside, it has not made her feel inside as whole, finished, organized, and unified as the outside image. She sheds the outer trappings, the costume of her transformation, her rented jewels, with coldly painful sarcasm, saying she does not wish to be accused of stealing; it is only the ring Henry bought her on an outing to Brighton that she is reluctant to remove, and this she retrieves from the fireplace only after he has left the room. ("Rich fashionable robes her person deck,/Pendants her ears, and pearls adorn her neck:/Her taper'd fingers too with rings are grac'd,/And an embroider'd zone surrounds her slender waste" [Ovid].) Eliza was full of despair and disappointment at the limitations of the "treatment." But she did not yet know that she in fact had had an effect on her "analyst" and had the ability to hurt him by her anger and her departure.

From his work with handicapped children, Duez has observed that every developmental gain represents simultaneously a loss: "When one succeeds at taking children from the supine to the sitting position, verticalized, this creates two things: on the one side, as one has invested a great deal and vigorously interpreted how good the sitting position is, a great pleasure is created, but at the same time a great distress, because all of the spatial references are put into question. . . . One finds, therefore, massive depressive moods" (1996, 128; my translation).[7] After the reception at the embassy—when she has seen a beautiful mirror image of herself in the eyes of high society—then she knows for certain that what she had "gotten" has left her even unhappier than she was when she started. By becoming the mirror image that she so desired, Eliza has entirely lost her familiar world. She wanders around Covent Garden, becoming even more acutely aware of the distance between her new and former selves/images. She has learned a most painful lesson from her brief visit to the territory of the Other.

It is then that she walks away from the mirror. Perhaps Henry and Pickering do her a favor when they do not pet or admire her (as Mrs. Higgins later tells them they should have), for it is the pain of not receiving this admiration that propels Eliza into self-analysis. Their failure perhaps constituted an optimal frustration because it allowed her to mature and to begin to internalize the regulation of her self-esteem. She interprets to herself that she does not need the mirror (Henry) any longer, she has the insight that it was Colonel Pickering's respect that was the "beginning of self-respect for me," and she speaks with ironic strength about her predicament. Yet, she has in fact found, if not a mirror, then a certain kind of ally in Henry's mother. As Kohut has pointed out, the need for selfobjects is lifelong. Interestingly, Shaw has depicted none of the interactions between the two that have resulted in their (therapeutic) alliance, in which the desire of the mother has functioned as a third element, giving Eliza needed refuge from the harsh world of the paternal law. We need both empathy and objectivity, both the imaginary and the symbolic, both mother and father.

Like all gains in analysis, though, Eliza's need further consolidation. At the unexpected sight of her father, she discovers that she is more apt to utter on old "A-a-a-a-ahowah" than she had realized, and in the long and heated exchange with Henry, she is still vulnerable, and feels swayed by his need of her. Her powerful moment of independence occurs, however, when she realizes that he cannot take away what he has given her—knowledge. She says, essentially, that she can be her own analyst. She realizes, too, that she may be lacking, but that he is as well; Eliza may not possess the phallus but neither does Henry. She demonstrates this achievement of insight and growth in a remarkable dialogue with her teacher. She makes a grammatical error, he corrects her, and she accepts his correction. A bit later she makes an error and corrects herself, demonstrating that she has internalized the "analytic" function. A further error that he points out leads her to exclaim, "I'll speak as I like. You're not my teacher now!" At this Henry smiles; whether his pleasure reflects pride in his own work or empathic appreciation for her claiming of her own autonomy, we can only guess. Yet it is probably a predominantly narcissistic moment, for later when Eliza declares herself to be his equal and his competitor, his response is wounded indignation. "If you can preach, I can teach," she says (essentially conferring upon herself the status of training analyst!).[8] And the significance of her intention here is that she has accepted that there is no magic to having "gotten it," to having attained the phallus.

As Henry has previously said, "heaven help the master who's judged by his disciples." He must return to his defensive position, both trying to assert ownership of Eliza's transformation and recasting it in phallic terms:

> Henry: By George, Eliza, I said I'd make a woman of you, and I have. I like you like this.
>
> Eliza: Yes, you may come to me now that I'm not afraid of you and can do without you.
>
> Henry: Of course I do, you little fool. Five minutes ago you were a millstone 'round my neck. Now you're a tower of strength, a consort battleship.
>
> Eliza: Goodbye, Professor Higgins.

For Henry, the crisis is generated by his intrapsychic conflict about affect. So scornful of emotion was he that he described Eliza's anguish about her fate as "purely subjective." At the tea party, both he and Pickering describe Eliza as an object, as an experiment; they cannot contain their excitement as they both bombard Mrs. Higgins with details of what a good pupil Eliza is. And yet there was at that point only the sense of Eliza as the beautiful statue, the object of their creation. It is not until the penultimate scene that Eliza claims for herself the ability to be aggressive toward Henry and Pickering, establishing the right to her own subjectivity. The intriguing question, of course, is whether Eliza's growth represents an uncovering of something that was already there or an entirely new creation, possible only in the context of this particular "analytic" relationship and set of circumstances. From what we know of Eliza's background, Henry and Pickering would certainly appear to have provided new object-relationships (Loewald 1960).

What was the mechanism of "cure," the manner in which the change took place? The "patient's" account in the penultimate scene begins with the way Pickering treated her:

> Eliza: Will you drop me all together now the experiment is over, Colonel Pickering?
>
> Pickering: Oh, you mustn't think of it as an experiment.
>
> Eliza: Oh, I'm only a "squashed cabbage leaf." [Henry slams down a newspaper in anger.] But I owe so much to you that I should be very unhappy if you forgot me. You see, it was from you that I learned really nice manners, and that's what makes one a lady, isn't it?
>
> Henry: Ha.
>
> Eliza: That's what makes the difference after all.
>
> Pickering: No doubt. Still, he taught you to speak and I couldn't have done that, you know.
>
> Eliza: Of course, that was his profession. It was just like learning to dance in the fashionable way. There was nothing more to it than that. But do you know what began my real education?
>
> Pickering: No.
>
> Eliza: Your calling me Miss Doolittle that day when I first came to Wimpole Street. That was the beginning of self-respect for me. You see, the difference between a lady and a flower girl isn't how she behaves, but how she's treated. I know that I shall always be a flower girl to Professor Higgins because he always treats me like a flower girl and always will.

This dialogue foreshadows the positions of both Kohut and Lacan, describing the importance of both the maternal and paternal functions, of empathy and objectivity—in short, the pain and the potential of the mirror.

But later in this scene when Eliza is speaking less defensively and aggressively, we learn that it was also the relationship with Henry that motivated her: "What I done, what I did, was not for the dresses and the taxis: I did it because we were pleasant together and I come—came—to care for you; not to want you to make love to me, and not forgetting the difference between us, but more friendly like."[9] Here, just as in clinical psychoanalysis, what brings the patient to treatment, the initial discomfort that prompts the request for help, is usually not the factor that keeps the patient in treatment, tolerating the discomfort of the work. It is the relationship with the analyst, and very often it is the more pre-Oedipal dyadic elements that are the most powerful. As Winnicott (1965) wrote, it can be the setting that is as important as the interpretations.

There is a series of triads in the structure of the story that deal with the elements of social desirability, morality, and conscience. Perhaps the most important of these has to do with language, for both Eliza and Henry are in agreement that proper pronunciation constitutes something desirable. As it does for the baby, language (the name/no of the father, *le nom/non du père*) serves to disrupt the imaginary and wordless communication with the mother. But it is a necessary separation without which the child could not truly enter the social world. For Eliza, her new speech will create an irrevocable separation from her roots; she will no longer speak her mother tongue, as it were. At other points in the story, it is Henry who seems to be living in the world of the imaginary, and others must lay down the law to him, must restrain his impulses and his sense that there are no boundaries. Note that at Mrs. Higgins's tea party, Henry is aghast at Eliza's behavior even as he not-so-secretly enjoys the way in which she disrupts the complacency of nice society. Both Mrs. Higgins and Mrs. Pearce lecture him about proper manners (after all, with a name like Pearce, it's got to be phallic!) and Colonel Pickering initially stands as the guardian of sexual propriety regarding Eliza. Later, Mrs. Higgins criticizes both his manners and his failure in empathy toward Eliza. And although there are moments when Henry treats Eliza with empathy, it is Colonel Pickering who provides the kindness and respect that she eventually internalizes; perhaps we should call this function the *oui*/we of the mother (Levine 1997).

But we can also question whether learning a structure, proper pronunciation, and etiquette (for instance how to address various dignitaries and royalty) created a change within the mind. Does psychoanalytic treatment work neurologically, from the outside in? Certainly this is related to Lacan's point, that all we do in analysis is work with signifiers, and that we are, in fact, all of us created by signifiers and by the system of signifiers. We are created, in other words, by the images from outside and are obligated to construe ourselves in relation to the other. Although the index to Lacan's work lists no reference to Pygmalion (Clark 1988), in his seminal 1949 paper, "The Mirror Stage as Formative of the Function of the I as Revealed in Psychoanalytic Experience," Lacan equates the alienating identification with the falsely whole mirror image (that is, the imago or the I) with "the statue in which man projects himself" (Lacan 1977, 2). He thus supports Bergmann's contention that the statue represents Pygmalion himself. Duez (1996, 128) elaborates the irony of the mirror: "[The mirror is] part of the real, but it is above all a human product: it is man who invented this surface where one can contemplate oneself. It is a symbolic organization of a Real that opens the specificity of the specular. Verticality is the signature of the subjectivising human position" (my translation).[10] The origin of the mirror, of course, is in that other ancient myth of psychoanalysis, that of Narcissus.

Curtain Call

I set out to write this "play" with several firm ideas in mind about what I wanted to say; but all the same, of course, I could not quite imagine what the finished product would look like. It is perhaps not coincidental that this was a troublesome essay, surprising me at almost each turn with what was appearing in its text. This particular experience of creation was striking in the degree to which I felt myself to be but a passive participant. Was this because of the ambivalence I have about the aggression of the creative process, the molding, the decisiveness, the desire? Or perhaps it was that my statue was not as beautiful as the one I imagined creating? My thoughts kept returning to the image of Michelangelo "finding" his bound slaves in the marble—a more grandiose comparison could scarcely be found, I admit! Nevertheless, as I write of Pygmalion and Henry Higgins I have perhaps joined their ranks, having labored to give birth to this brainchild. As Miller points out, "storytelling itself is also an ethical act involving personification for which the storyteller must be held responsible, as must reader, teacher, or critic for bringing the story to life by reading it, talking about it, writing about it" (1990, viii). And so I offer this story to you, asking you to give it life yourself by finding it useful, interesting, or even beautiful. But am I Henry here, or Eliza? Artist or statue? Analyst or analysand? For you can "see" my thoughts while I cannot "see" yours.

Notes

1. For consistency with the Pygmalion story as well as for ease of reading I will designate the patient as female and the analyst as male.

2. A further coincidence: Both Freud and George Bernard Shaw were born in 1856.

3. My translation of the French, "consistence."

4. "Il peut être le premier horizon de Galatée (ou le premier horizon, le premier paysage de l'enfant est bien le corps maternal penché sur lui) en même temps que l'amant. Dès lors, le fantasme qu'il soulève n'est-il pas celui d'être tout pour l'objet, de remplacer, et par là-même d'exclure, tous les objets de l'objet?" (1997, 178). *He can be the first horizon for Galatea (now the first horizon, the first landscape of*

the baby is certainly the mother's body bending over him) at the same time as the lover. From that moment, the fantasy that it raises, isn't it to be everything for the object, to replace, and in that very place to exclude all other objects from the object? (My translation)

5. "Pygmalion se décolle de son oeuvre en passant de la position de créateur à celle de récepteur" (1997, 179). *Pygmalion separates (literally: unglues) himself from his work in moving from the position of creator to that of receiver.* (My translation)

6. Margulies (1993, 55) writes of this in a most elegant and moving way, describing how the (undisclosed) death of his father was reflected in his patients' material. "In the circularity of empathy and in the resonance of our unconscious overlap, *I empathize with another—and am startled to find myself*" (Margulies' emphasis).

7. "Quand on réussit à passer les enfants de la position allongée à la position assise, verticalisée, cela crée deux choses: d'une part comme on a beaucoup investi et interprété violemment que cela irait tellement bien en position assise, se crée une grande jouissance, mais en même temps une grand détresse, car tous les référents spaciaux sont mise en cause. . . . On rencontre alors des dépositions dépressives massives."

8. In fact, the creation fantasy may be a particular danger in the unique and peculiar instance of the training analysis.

9. Perhaps the movie ought to have been called *My Frère Lady.*

10. "[Le miroir est] une part de réel, mais c'est avant tout une production humaine: ce sont les hommes qui ont inventé cette surface où l'on peut se réfléchir. C'est une organisation symbolique d'un Réel qui ouvre le spécificité du spéculaire. La verticalité est la signature de la position subjectivante humaine."

Catching the Wrong Leopard

Courage and Masochism in the Psychoanalytic Situation

2

IN THE 1938 HOWARD HAWKS COMEDY *Bringing Up Baby*, Katharine Hepburn's character (named Susan!) finds herself in a most precarious position. In her effort to find her aunt's escaped, tame leopard ("Baby"), she has inadvertently captured the leopard that a nearby circus had deemed too dangerous to keep. Thinking it is Baby, she manages to get a rope around its neck and tugs it all the way to the police station, where Cary Grant's character, David, awaits her. We hear her muttering to the leopard, "Oh, what's the matter with you? You've been slapping at me the whole way." Upon her arrival, she says to Cary Grant: "Well, did I fool you this time—you thought I was doing the wrong thing, but I've got him!" He responds: "No, you haven't, Susan!"

Was the capture courageous? Did she know, and simultaneously not allow herself to know, of the danger she was in? Might we not wonder about an element of masochism in her determination? Is it ever possible to know if the leopards we catch are, in fact, tame?

Full of distress, hope, the wish to be changed, and the wish to remain the same, patients may have little awareness of the leopards they are dragging when they first seek help from us. When Katharine Hepburn sees the leopard she thought was Baby, she realizes that she has caught the wrong leopard, and she is overcome by terror. Cary Grant picks up a chair and uses it to maneuver the leopard into an empty jail cell. Is this not what we analysts also do? And is the psychoanalytic process not helped along at times by our sense of humor and our expectation that wonderful transformations may emerge from the absurd or the tragic? Do we not help our patients confront, cage, and tame the unruly things they discover?

I am repeatedly impressed by the way in which almost every patient entering psychoanalysis and psychotherapy experiences a similar predicament, and by how the issue reemerges at points when new areas of pain or conflict become apparent. And the courage-masochism experience is taking place not solely in our patients. Unlike the hapless Cary Grant, who, in high Hollywood 1930s madcap mode, was swept into Katharine Hepburn's sphere, we analysts know full well that we are going to be encountering untamed leopards of one sort or another. If analysis works, patients and analysts will always be getting into more than they originally bargained for. The psychoanalytic situation inevitably must evoke both courage and masochism in us as well.

This chapter will introduce the subject of courage into the psychoanalytic discourse about masochism and will also demonstrate that ordinary ethical and axiological concerns can and should be included in our psychoanalytic language and practice. We want our patients to be courageous enough to do the work of analysis, and it is disingenuous to pretend otherwise. As Olsson (1994) writes: "In our efforts to refrain from moralizing or being judgmental, sometimes in our therapeutic work we act as if the in-depth exploration of morality or helping the analysand to make judgments about their morality, its roots, and their rebellion about it, were off-limits for the analytic process" (35).

We analysts, too, need to have what Balint (1957) termed "'the courage of one's own stupidity.' This means the doctor feels free to be himself with his patient—that is, to use all his past experiences and present skills without much inhibition" (305). Why do analysts speak to each other so rarely about courage and similar positive values or qualities and about whether we talk about these with patients? I wonder whether there is a reluctance to speak about such "unscientific" things as values and about the ways in which psychoanalysis is a profoundly beautiful and moral endeavor. Analysts are also reluctant, I think, to make observations that may seem too supportive and complimentary to the patient (or to ourselves). However, it is equally important to interpret what is positive or progressive as what is negative and regressive. Defenses and resistances serve a positive need—self-protection. It is important for patients to understand that even the most inefficient, destructive, or masochistic defense must have represented the individual's best and most courageous attempt at adaptation.

Likewise, we should interpret, when appropriate, what seems to be courageous—and we should be curious about the ways in which it also serves masochistic needs. At each stage of an analysis, it may be helpful to clarify to the patient the uncertainty in his or her mind about the ways in which taking a step deeper into the analytic relationship is both courageous and masochistic. This can open the door to exploration of conscious beliefs and how they relate to unconscious fantasies and assumptions. Considering the possibility that even a sadomasochistic enactment simultaneously represents a courageous attempt to rework conflict or trauma will help us listen in a more balanced way to both manifest and latent material. I try to keep this in mind from the very first moments of a treatment.

A patient who had had a previous frustrating and demoralizing treatment was considering entering analysis with me. She asked me whether it could really help her. I answered that sometimes analysis is not helpful at all, but that it could also be transformative in ways that neither she nor I could imagine at that moment. My honesty included both the possibility that her masochism would be gratified and that her courage would pay off.

Kohut's Contributions to the Study of Courage

Kohut is one of the few psychoanalytic writers to have addressed the subject of courage at length. An examination of his thinking will highlight the question of whether we can consider courage to exist without accompanying masochism. In his essay "On Courage" (1985), Kohut relates courage to what he terms the nuclear self. He defines courage as "the ability to brave death and to tolerate destruction rather than betray the nucleus of one's psychological being, that is, one's ideals" (6). To talk about ideals in Kohutian terms, though, is not to speak of the ego ideal and the superego, but rather to enter a discourse about the nuclear self: "[T]he carrier of the derivatives of the grandiose-exhibitionistic self [and] . . . the self which has set its sights on values and ideals which are the descendents of the idealized parent imago" (35). Kohut connects this notion of the nuclear self to his concept of Tragic Man, arguing that it is within the grasp of most people to achieve a "modicum of self-realization" (48).

Kohut (1985) sets out to answer what it is that "allows (or compels)" (5) some individuals to defend their beliefs to this ultimate degree. He selects as illustrations remarkable Germans who were killed as a result of their refusal to go along with Nazism. Heroic courage, he argues, involves the individual's capacity to experience and work through inner conflict of monumental dimensions (15); the action thus reflects the individual's ideal(ism). Kohut makes a distinction between the "martyr-hero" and the "rational resister," based on the degree to which courage is "predominantly determined by the cognitive functions of [the] ego" (22–23).

Although some may argue that Kohut is better understood on his own terms, I am not certain that he truly addresses the question he himself raised when he asks whether there is a compulsion to behave heroically. What created the drive in these particular individuals to resist the Nazis; could this possibly have been exclusively related to self-realization in a way that is entirely free of aggression?

Kohut (1981) describes the moment of death of one of these heroic German figures, Sophie Scholl,[1] who had a dream on the eve of her execution that she had managed to protect a baby from grave danger, but had lost her life in the process. "Her cheeks were flushed with vitality when she was executed. *This is not a hysterical fantasy of a masochistic nature.* This is someone alive for a cause that will live on; that baby was placed on the other side of a crevasse as she was falling. And she said: 'It's all right, the baby will live on.' So is this optimism? Maybe" (1981, 223, italics added).

I question Kohut's assertion and whether this remarkable woman's vitality may in fact represent a denial of the grim reality of the bodily death awaiting her. I am aware that I cannot enter her psyche. But nor can Kohut, and it is reasonable to assume that some masochistic element was being gratified simultaneously with the admirable refusal to compromise her principles. What is noteworthy, however, is that Kohut has raised the subject of masochism in his essay on courage.

As Coles (1965) and Novick and Novick (1987) point out, there is a relationship between feelings of omnipotence and acts of either courage or masochism. (I will discuss these authors' work later.) Perhaps Kohut believes that Sophie Scholl had so thoroughly worked through her anxiety that she could greet death with vitality and with certainty that it would be all right because the baby would survive; however, some manifestation of a struggle to relinquish self-preservative instincts would go farther to convince me that her act was characterized by courage as opposed to fearlessness (Rachman 1984). In any case, Kohut's assertion that there existed no component of masochistic fantasy in Scholl's act does not seem to me to be justified by his description of her appearance and her dream.

Nonetheless, it is Kohut's hypothesis that heroism involves so intense an identification with one's ideals that the life of the body carries a vastly reduced significance. For him, this marks the ultimate expression of the nuclear self. In this argument and in his larger metapsychology, Kohut's view of aggression as a breakdown product, as a result solely of empathic failure, is not without controversy. But even if we agree to accept this view, it is unlikely that anyone escapes childhood experiencing only such minimal empathic failures on the part of caregivers as to permit avoidance of the establishment of some form of aggression within the psyche. Such aggression may be turned against the self under certain environmental conditions. Can we go as far as Kohut does, to accept his view that there can exist mental states in which aggression plays no role whatsoever—and that there could exist a courageous state that would not simultaneously gratify some unconscious masochism?

Courage, Masochism, and the Psychoanalytic Discourse

Courage, while clearly understood as an inner quality of mind, is usually considered in terms of its social manifestations, from an objective perspective. We have come to associate courage as much with its valued result as with the mental quality that fuels the action. It is interesting to note that the etymological root of courage is the Latin *cor*—heart.[2]

I understand courage to refer to a conscious decision to tolerate risk or pain for the purpose of achieving a higher goal. This is where the issue of values enters the picture, for we associate courage with aims that are generally agreed to be of moral value or good; we refer to it as a value because it is objectively valued. For analysts, it is the subjective understanding, rather than objective behavior, that determines our assessments.[3]

For example, if a man rushes into a burning house to rescue $100,000 in cash from the flames, we would be more likely to consider this courageous if he plans to donate this money to charity than if he plans to use it to buy a Porsche for himself. Yet perhaps the Porsche buyer is so narcissistically fragile that his very sense of self may be at stake without the car. Conversely, if we look at the well-known example of the impoverished man who robs a pharmacy to obtain vital medication for his dying wife, we could easily devise a scenario (for instance, guilt over extramarital affairs) that would render this action less clearly courageous or morally admirable. While psychoanalysts assume that manifest masochism is a derivative of deeper unconscious trends, this same consideration has only occasionally been accorded to the concept of courage. I am suggesting that we must find a way of expanding our psychoanalytic metapsychology and phenomenology to encompass concepts such as courage that are ordinarily considered to be part of the discourse of common language.[4]

Other analysts and clinicians besides Kohut have addressed the issue of courage. Coles (1965), for example, writes that considering the question of courage helped him see the people of the American South whom he studied "in some coherent psychological perspective" (89). He also addresses the larger question of whether mental health professionals have adequately considered issues such as courage, pointing out that critics have characterized "bravery, sacrifice, heroism, and continuing good will" as "other psychological events" (Coles 1965, 86), somehow beyond the stuff of psychological suffering to which mental health professionals usually attend: "We are accused of being intent on unmasking the false and pretentiously 'moral,' and thereby overlooking the possibility of a genuinely ethical quality to man's thinking and behavior" (86). I wonder whether this ethical element may be based in the capacity for empathy. If so, then courageous behavior, as well as its lack or its opposite, could be adequately accounted for by our psychoanalytic developmental theory (that is to say, insofar as any human function can be adequately accounted for by rational understanding).

Anna Freud (1956) places the issue of courage in the context of the psychoanalytic discourse on the nature of anxiety:

> Most analytic authors insist that, by the working of our mind, external danger is inevitably and automatically transformed into internal threats, i.e., that all fear is in the last resort anxiety with regard to id events. Personally, I find it difficult to subscribe to this sweeping statement. I believe in a sliding scale between external and internal threats and fears. What we call "courage" in ordinary language is, I believe, no more than the individual's ability to deal with external threats on their own ground and prevent the bulk of them from joining forces with the manifold dangers lurking in the id (431).

I would add here, however, that every external event or action would necessarily have significance to the individual, even if the event does not represent an enactment of an already existing internal conflict.

Fenichel (1945) points out the relationship between what appears to others as courage and the counterphobic attitude. And Coles (1965) captures the complexity of the issue: "Much of what might properly be called courage can be understood in the light of what we know about conflicted minds. Guilt and the need for punishment, the promptings of exhibitionistic needs, narcissistic trends which tell a person that he is immortal or indestructible, that even somehow evoke ecstasy under danger, all of these neurotic personality developments may be found as determinants of courageous behavior" (96–97).

Moore and Fine (1990) hold that the pleasure/displeasure of masochism is most often unconscious, except in cases of masochistic perversions (116), and their definition also stresses that the specific goal of the suffering is a sexual one. Although I am in this chapter considering characterological and moral masochism, rather than the masochism found in specific perversions, it is in a sense spurious to make categorical distinctions; Freud (1924, 169) points out the connection between moral masochism and sexuality. Novick and Novick (1987) propose the following concise but comprehensive definition: "Masochism is the active pursuit of psychic or physical pain, suffering, or humiliation in the service of adaptation, defense, and instinctual gratification at oral, anal, and phallic levels" (381).

The term masochism has entered common parlance, as I will discuss below; analysts, however, usually use the term to refer to an inferred psychological state—in other words, an understanding from the perspective of the patient's subjectivity (possibly on a metapsychological level) of the motivation of actions. (Sometimes, however, masochism requires no greater level of inference than does courage—for instance, in the case of those perversions that involve the enjoyment of pain.) As I have often remarked to patients, the curious thing is that courage does not necessarily feel very good in the moment of the act and the risk; conversely, masochistic acts may not always engender conscious displeasure (although they often do). Perhaps this is not curious, for masochism and courage may share an affective tone of suspenseful anxiety. There is a similarity in the conscious affect produced, for it is the presence of an element of risk that characterizes both the courageous and the masochistic act. How is one to distinguish "worthwhile risk" (Maleson 1984, 336) from masochistic strivings? One answer to this question is that in masochism, the painful state itself represents the aim, while in courage it represents the means to an end.

Loewenstein (1957) addresses a similar point: "Although it was an important discovery of psychoanalysis that masochism may lead an individual unconsciously to seek suffering and failure, this does not justify us to attribute every suffering or failure to masochistic strivings. External reality is not a mere projection of the individual's instinctual drives" (211).

Thinking about masochism colloquially rather than technically affords us another opportunity to be attuned to the way patients consciously understand their experiences and motivations. Many people label as masochistic, or as self-destructive, a self-initiated action that results in a painful outcome; there is a tendency to feel as though one has done it to oneself. Likewise, the courageous individual is not unconscious of risk or immune to its affective significance. The affective experience of courage, however, may feel as though one is subjecting oneself to punishment, even when one does the "right" thing—the avoidance of unpleasure remains a powerful motivational force even when we have (more or less) attained the reality principle in our mental functioning.

Courage can be seen as a superego quality (Brenner 1996) linked to the ego ideal, to the ambitions toward which one strives as well as to the desire to avoid punishment—the prohibitions internalized in the mind. Both the assessment of reality and the awareness of one's internal world are obviously critical elements in courageous acts, in that fear is related to both external and internal consequences of one's actions. The role of the superego in self-evaluation cannot be easily distinguished from the ego's function of self-observation (Stein 1966); thus, the superego is closely implicated in reality testing and in the assessment of risk. We must also distinguish fearlessness from courage (Rachman 1984).

While some observers may believe that the pain associated with masochism constitutes the goal of the behavior, Berliner (1940) suggests that, quite to the contrary, masochistic behavior may have its roots in desperate attempts to maintain a loving relationship with a sadistic object. Novick and Novick (1987, 377) suggest that beating fantasies may be an effort to invoke the desired (but in reality absent) strong father who can control the impulses toward destruction. (This is remarkably consistent with Lacan's notion of the name of the father, the paternal metaphor that emancipates the child from maternal engulfment and permits triadicfunctioning.[5]) It is possible to imagine, therefore, a way in which there may be an element of courage and hope in all masochistic acts, in the sense in which Winnicott (1963) discovered hope in the antisocial symptom. Although Freud derived the concept of the death instinct from the repetition compulsion, perhaps there is a way to re-view repetition and masochism as representing hope and courage—just as I am suggesting that we increase our cynicism and seek the underlying masochism in courage.[6]

Ghent (1990), in his consideration of the relationship between masochism, submission, and surrender, points out that masochistic character and object relations may represent an attempt to repeat and thus integrate experience that was initially indigestible. I would understand this to mean an experience that was traumatic, that overwhelmed the capacities of the ego, that the child was not able to render into symbolic terms (that is, symbolic in the Lacanian sense; Ghent does not use this language). Relying heavily on Winnicott's concept of impingement and on his distinction between object relations and object usage, Ghent writes of surrender not in terms of loss but rather of gain, of opening oneself to the potential of one's true self (recall Kohut's nuclear self) and to external influences: "The intensity of the masochism is a living testimonial of the urgency with which some buried part of the personality is screaming to be exhumed" (116). And later: "I am suggesting that some instances of masochism may be rooted in a deep quest for understanding, for undoing the isolation" (127).

Ghent's paper is relevant not only for its specific conclusions, but also for its methodology. He is attempting, as I am, to speak psychoanalytically about topics not normally thought to be within the purview of our field, and to find kernels of healthy striving in masochism. Ghent also points to the masochism and surrender inherent in the work of the analyst (133). Through our surrendering to the empathic experiencing of our patients' pain and to the many frankly painful experiences within the therapeutic relationship, we are able both to mitigate patients' suffering and to grow ourselves. Quoting Yeats, Ghent urges us to "tread softly" on patients' masochism and submissiveness, advice with which I concur.

I realize that, in a formal sense, I am mixing frames of reference when I maintain that if we analyze any instance of what, colloquially, we call courage, we will find an element of masochism, and if we analyze any instance of what, psychoanalytically, we call masochism, we will find an effort at courageous mastery. However, in my view, our psychoanalytic terminology is no more privileged in terms of objectivity than is the language of morals and values. When we speak about masochism, we use a construct to make sense of a behavior or of a mental state. And we do the same when we speak about courage. The difference between the two terms is that one, centuries-old, has become part of ordinary language. We tend to think of courage less as an abstraction than as a simple label. But masochism, a concept we recognize as an abstraction, is as much a label as is courage; it is also just a word, with no referent that possesses a time-space reality. Masochism simply addresses a more recent concept, and one whose referent may be less easily identifiable. But neither term, courage nor masochism, possesses the same potential for empirical verification as does a description of brown hair or a broken arm. I believe we must reconsider the extent to which our use of a purportedly neutral psychoanalytic language may in fact be much less objective, value-free, or scientific than we think (see, for instance, Barratt 1994 and Mitchell 1998).

A search of the literature has revealed but one article explicitly addressing the subject of courage and masochism. Prince (1974) identifies a number of facets of clinical work that demand a courageous attitude on the part of the therapist. I would argue, though, that it is as much masochism as courage that influences the willingness of some clinicians to endure the rigors of clinical work. While Prince eloquently describes the responsibility of the clinician to eschew the orthodox or clichéd behavior in favor of the creative and courageous clinical intervention, he relies on a definition of masochism so little explored as to dilute the impact of his thoughts. My own clinical experience has led me to agree with Prince that the creativity of the therapeutic decision does demand courage. I differ from him in that I would not necessarily characterize the failure to act creatively or courageously as masochistic—as a "flight"—as he does. What Prince defines as the analyst's masochism ("a flight from individualized creative responses with an illusion of autonomy supported by a fetishistic attachment to putative analytic ideals" [48]) I might be inclined to categorize as cowardice.

There are many reasons why therapists may not make the sort of intervention that Prince describes: fear of disapproval, mediocrity, lack of creativity or mental giftedness, or the inability to think beyond one's training or beyond a single theoretical orientation. These are not invariably synonymous with masochism, undesirable as these qualities may be in a clinician. If a therapist, on the other hand, is aware of what specific unconventional response the situation seems to demand, if that therapist is relatively certain that his or her judgment is free of inappropriate countertransference, and then if the therapist does not opt to take this step, I might tend to focus on the possible presence of sadism toward the patient as much as on the therapist's own masochism.[7]

Cowardice might function as a defense against this sadism. What Prince is describing may be better described as a failure to act with integrity than as masochism. My focus is different from Prince's, too, in that I am suggesting that the masochism is embedded in the clinician's decision to be creative, to take the risk, to act with integrity in accord with what that clinical situation appears to demand.

Prince also argues that "the core of psychotherapeutic courage is to face and deal with one's inner experiences of being a therapist" (49); that "the capacity for empathy involves the courage to risk fluid boundaries" (55); and that one aspect of our work that is most difficult to bear is uncertainty, specifically, the "courageous attitude that is produced by the necessity of the therapist having to endure being the target of the patient's transference" (52). All these points are correct—but they are incomplete. For each of these demands upon the therapist or analyst will simultaneously involve a masochistic response as well. Sometimes, as when we must tolerate rage in the transference from a borderline patient, our masochism is quite conscious; we know that treating this kind of patient will entail this sort of experience.[8] But all relationships of caring or love involve a degree of masochism, insofar as we are willing to sacrifice our own interests for those of the loved one.

Clinical Applications

In almost every psychoanalysis and psychotherapy, I see the patient experience some degree of intertwined courage and masochism. It occurs often at the beginning of therapy or analysis, as well as at junctures in the treatment when patients are at the brink of exploring material that will clearly be painful, or of deepening their trust in the analyst. It is particularly intense in patients who have histories of early trauma or poor object relationships with early caregivers. The most acute instances I have seen are when a patient comes to me after a previous, unsuccessful analysis or therapy. The following vignette is unusual only in that it demonstrates a moment of intertwined courage and masochism in the analyst as well as in the patient, and in that my intervention involved a clarification that was rather confrontational.

Clinical Illustration

A man in his late twenties sought analysis for anxiety and depression from which he had suffered for as long as he could remember. Fred was becoming increasingly aware that the series of jobs he had worked at since college left him with no career to speak of, and earning much less money than he would have liked at a time when he and his wife had decided to start a family.

The central fantasy Fred reported in the first weeks of analysis was an image of being in a dark and shut-off place, alone and frightened. Although there did exist a potential way to exit this place, the patient expressed the thought that perhaps he had been in this place so long that its familiarity discouraged him from even wanting to leave. I understood this to be a self-state fantasy that, I later came to believe, had predicted the specific manifestation of the courage-masochism predicament the analysis would stimulate. Counterbalancing this ominous image was the fact of Fred's excruciating discomfort with his state of mind most of the time; his desire to change was initially quite strong.

A few months into the analysis, Fred modified this fantasy. He reported that, contrary to his first description, the access to the potential exit was not clear. He added that he did not want me to disapprove if he decided he did not want to leave this place at all in the end. I commented to the patient that I was struck by the complex position he wished me to fill in his mind, that he needed me both to want him to feel better—to be invested in his doing well—and simultaneously not to disapprove if he did not want to do better or did not have the courage to try to leave the place he described.

Fred became quite preoccupied with the issue of courage. He revealed that, for years, he had questioned whether he possessed this quality; my remark had been so painful that it practically felt as though I had betrayed him, he said. I think this pain resulted from my having articulated something Fred had been afraid to voice—the question of whether he was a coward. The patient and I were then able to speak quite directly about the familiarity of the terrible place as a resistance to his conscious wishes to feel better. As Fred mused about this, he wondered whether he wanted to work to make himself into any particular character type (he mentioned an often-caricatured politician), or whether he would "just like to be like Fred."

In the following session, the patient commented that he did not quite understand what had happened, but that it felt as though the earth had shifted a bit. Although there had been times in his life when he had felt all right about himself, more or less, he said, he had never before thought of himself by name or seen possible value in being just himself. Fred added that this was a new and unfamiliar feeling.

My introduction of the issue of courage seemed to have functioned for the patient as a confrontation, a kind of challenge, and an acknowledgment of his long-held but unspoken concerns. As painful as this was for Fred, it was probably also an enormous relief to be able to acknowledge what amounted to a proverbial elephant in the room. What did my intervention do? What was the significance of the patient's use of his own name? My hypothesis is that this patient wanted me to be the dyadic partner in what Lacan would call the register of the imaginary, that world of wordless communication inhabited by mother and child. However, Fred also needed me to function as the name of the father, the paternal metaphor that disrupts the imaginary and insists that the child function in the social world, which is represented by the triad and is characterized by the use of language. Lacan terms this the symbolic register. Thus, the father's (and the analyst's) aggressive interruption of the imaginary is a developmentally necessary event (see, in this regard, Raphling 1992). By putting into words the impossible position he needed me to inhabit in his mind—that I should both want him to be better and not disapprove if he decided not to try to get better—I refused to gratify Fred's wish that I join him in the register of the imaginary. He thus reported the profound but confusing change in his sense of self, which led him to think of himself by name—that is to say, in the symbolic. In other words, when I demonstrated that I respected the law, the necessity of the symbolic register, so, too, could he make this shift. It is also possible that Fred's response represented a defense against considering whether I had condemned him as a coward.

How did I know that courage and masochism might be relevant to this patient when it was not a part of his manifest material? I think that I was sensitive to the possibility that that issue would arise from the moment he had originally revealed his fantasy.[9] Fred was struggling to sort out whether he had the courage to commit himself to the analysis, which he believed had the potential to help him get out of the terrible place that he inhabited. The process of leaving, though, Fred saw as threatening, and, therefore, it represented a masochistic as well as a courageous solution. Note that it was after he experienced my interpretation as so hurtful that he reported the tentative change in the way he was thinking of himself. Perhaps, as painful as this was to him, there was something familiar about being in a dependent relationship with an object he imagined to be sadistic. It does seem clear that the courageous solution had become infused somehow with a degree of masochism, that the experience of some masochistic/sadistic element in the analytic relationship established the condition for him to experience some growth—a gesture toward the exit. In other words, the effectiveness of the intervention was progressive insofar as it clarified a previously unarticulated feeling—but regressive insofar as the familiarity of being treated sadistically established the condition for change.[10] I did not interpret the enactment element to Fred, as it was not until this writing that I considered it. A reminder of Freud's (1919) comment about the fantasy of being beaten by one's father is apropos: "People who harbour phantasies of this kind develop a special sensitiveness and irritability towards anyone whom they can include in the class of fathers. They are easily offended by a person of this kind, and in that way (to their own sorrow and cost) bring about the realization of the imagined situation of being beaten by their father" (195).

By inferring and interpreting the patient's conflict concerning courage—and, by implication, his fear that he would be able to get himself out of the frightening place—I was introducing the personal and social question of values into the analytic arena. I was stating the forbidden, that I thought it would be better if he had the courage to do this, to help himself, or to accept my help. It is clear from Fred's response that this question had been troubling him for some time.

Did my intervention constitute a breach of the nonjudgmental analytic stance? I had never heard another analyst describe an interpretation on this level of discourse (Raphling 1995).[11] It is certainly possible that this was a less daring interpretation than I imagined it to be. But what is germane to an understanding of this interaction is that I did, in fact, imagine it to be a courageous intervention, and one that might lead to condemnation by my analytic supervisor (Fred was my first control case). Part of what led me to expect condemnation was, no doubt, the sadism in my intervention, an expression of the anger I felt at the possibility of this patient's ending his treatment. Insofar as I imagined condemnation (and condemned myself), my act was certainly masochistic as well.

I wondered, then, whether this was the sort of remark analysts do not talk about, because it flies in the face of one of the cardinal rules of our training—to be nonjudgmental and value-neutral in our approach to patients. But not to make this interpretation would have felt like a betrayal of my responsibility, an avoidance of the exploration of courage and values that was central to an understanding of my patient's painful predicament. And this predicament involved his question about his own cowardice.

We analysts are not neutral insofar as we actively wish for our patients to get better; we hope to help them. In the interaction described in this vignette, I believe I clarified the patient's conflict about his courage and confronted his passivity or cowardice. I revealed how much I value courage (and my lack of neutrality in this regard), as well as my wish to help Fred. That my intervention felt courageous to me is, in a sense, beside the point. I believe that my interest in the subject of courage and masochism helped me understand a conflict that already existed in this patient; however, the acts of clarification and observation inevitably influenced the data.

Conclusions

Courage is a vital dimension to which analysts should be attuned in their own experience and in regard to their patients' experiences. Clarification and interpretation of conflicts related to courage and other values and virtues, such as integrity, are within the proper and necessary scope of psychoanalysis. Judicious revelation of the analyst's own values may at times be appropriate, and, certainly, the analyst's values form a central part of the matrix of the helping relationship whether explicitly revealed or not. Some analysts may feel reluctant to introduce courage and other values into the analytic arena, believing that it is the role of the analyst to analyze, not to evaluate or to judge. However, we convey an evaluation, a form of judgment, whenever we share our observations of the patient—for instance, an observation about affects—with the patient, and patients depend on us for our honest willingness to look at all aspects, including the moral ones, of their lives.

It is particularly poignant to consider this topic at a time when psychoanalysis—and the psychoanalytic understanding of the mind—is under attack. Being (or becoming) an analyst nowadays is no longer an easy step along a royal road to success and respect from one's colleagues. It is a choice that itself embodies the conflict between, and concordance of, courage and masochism. And within psychoanalysis itself, we must negotiate theoretical and political disagreements among ourselves, even as we acknowledge the urgent need to convey to an increasingly skeptical public that our work is invaluable and irreplaceable.

Bollas (1987) argues that we have perhaps betrayed the most important of Freud's legacies in that we have not lived up to the standards of honesty and profound curiosity called for by Freud. He believes that we have not communicated the specific skills of using ourselves, along with our patients, as subject matter, in a way that has been persuasive to many in the "hard" sciences (as well as in the humanities). He notes both the courage (and possibly the masochism) of psychoanalytic pioneers:

> What is it about a Winnicott, a Bion or a Lacan—beyond simply their genius that is so inspiring these days? Why do we enjoy reading their works even if much of what is there to be read is elusive and strange? Can we simply say that such analytic writers appeal to us because they have acted out against a fundamental responsibility to remain psychoanalytically kosher, an acting out in which we slyly participate by proxy? I think not. It is my view that people are drawn to the works of such people because in them they find a daring, a *courage to be idiomatic* and to stay with the private creations of their analytic experience and life—a profoundly Freudian accomplishment on their part (238, italics in original).

A final thought remains. While in *Bringing Up Baby* it is Cary Grant's external response that confronts Katharine Hepburn with the courageous and masochistic nature of her act, much of the time we face our own triumphs and disasters privately. Why is it that one so seldom hears people talk about the personal experience of courage, despite the abundance of situations that require this quality in all of us? Does courage feel to us like humility, such that the very act of saying that one possesses it may mean one does not? Or is it perhaps an unconscious recognition that, in doing so, we would be revealing a substrate of masochism? Perhaps, in appearing to have acted courageously, we know that we have also caught the wrong leopard.

Notes

1. Although I cannot know what meaning, if any, this may have, I note that Kohut here refers to this woman as Marie, despite her identification as Sophie Scholl in his essay "On Courage" (1985).

2. A glance at past usages of courage reveals connections to both sexuality and aggression. An online version of the *Oxford English Dictionary* (2005) includes the following among its historical summary: "The heart as the seat of feeling, thought, etc.; spirit, mind, disposition, nature"; "What is in one's mind or thoughts, what one is thinking of or intending; intention, purpose; desire or inclination"; "Spirit, liveliness, lustiness, vigour, vital force or energy"; "Anger, wrath"; "Haughtiness, pride"; "Confidence, boldness"; "Sexual vigour and inclination; lust"; and "That quality of mind which shows itself in the facing of danger without fear or shrinking; bravery, boldness, valour." I thank Lisa Jarnot, M.F.A., for suggesting this reference to me.

3. I would like to comment here about the issue of analysts' making judgments and moral evaluations about patients. First of all, our very use of language involves evaluations. We use this word as opposed to that one when we speak to patients; we choose to comment on this association and not that one. These decisions that analysts make many times in every session involve evaluations about what is most important; we constantly make value judgments in this way. Further, these judgments, evaluations, or diagnostic assessments are inherent in our subjective, psychoanalytic listening. We wonder as we listen: What does this mean? We try out various hypotheses in our minds before sharing them with patients. I assume that my listening is infused with my values—even if those values are nothing more than what I would consider a benevolent valuing of health and self-knowledge. But I do not assume that I can know which other values or morals may be embedded in my responses. Thus, I believe it is better to be open about the fact that we make judgments, rather than to pretend that we are capable of listening without doing so. I know that I do evaluate, as I listen, whether actions and thoughts a patient reports to me might represent changes in a narcissistic state, actings out, resistances, and so forth.

4. Lest we analysts become uneasy about a seemingly too high-minded discussion of courage, we need only remind ourselves of the lustful and earthy links embodied in colloquial synonyms for courageous, such as ballsy and gutsy. Courage is linked to mind, heart, digestive system, and testicles.

5. The main point here is that there is an attempt in the masochistic position, as described by Novick and Novick, to continue the process of development and the structuring of the mind. Lacan offers a different view of mental structure, seeing the registers of the imaginary, the symbolic, and the real as more broadly expansive than the categories of id, ego, and superego. For a summary of Lacanian concepts, see Levine 1996. I would like to stress that here, as well as in the clinical illustration, I do not intend my use of Lacanian theory to distract from the main subject of this chapter. As the reader will note, I draw on a variety of theories, ranging

from compromise formation through object relations to Lacanian. I believe that clinical work benefits when the analyst feels free to utilize whichever theory most aids understanding in a particular moment. As long as the analyst is comfortable in this, it should not lead to a disruptive or fragmented listening and interpretive stance.

6. Although Freud did not write at length about courage, he used the words courage or courageous sixty times in the *Standard Edition* (Parrish, Guttman, and Jones 1980). There is no occasion in which courage is mentioned in relation to masochism. However, the connection may not be too distant when Freud speaks of the intellectual courage involved in putting forth new ideas (insofar as an innovator can expect to receive the initial scorn and disbelief of colleagues). Issues of values and positive qualities were certainly alive in Freud's thinking. Olsson (1994) cites Freud's observation that "psycho-analytic treatment is founded on truthfulness" (Freud 1915, 164). I do not think we stretch Freud's meaning if we assume that he was aware of what Olsson (1994) later termed "the struggle and the challenge of truthfulness within the self" (35).

7. Rothstein (1995) goes as far as to tell patients reluctant to enter psychoanalysis that they are taking a masochistic position by denying themselves the best treatment possible. I believe that when clinicians decide not to confront a patient who is leaving treatment prematurely with the advantages of continuing, this may constitute masochism; when something may benefit clinicians (financially or emotionally), we may be reluctant to recognize and articulate the benefits to the patient.

8. In my chapter on the aesthetics of psychoanalysis, I described my way of thinking about these difficult episodes.

9. Then, too, my mind outside my clinical hours was occupied at the time with the creation of this essay. I must acknowledge experiencing some guilt at the moment of the interpretation, even before the patient responded. I was not unaware that I might in fact be eliciting material for this chapter, even as I was saying what I genuinely felt was appropriate and necessary in that moment. It could be that my guilt (over my sadistic "use" of Fred for my own needs) was the evoked partner of his possibly masochistic surrender to me (he did not respond to all interpretations in this fashion).

10. This treatment took place in the mid-1990s, before Cooper (2000) wrote of "perverse support" (8–9) and Smith (2000) of "benign negative countertransference" (95). Both authors illustrate interventions that, while not unempathic, jar or even provoke the patient into further self-observation.

11. This is obviously a good rule of thumb to maintain, and I am not suggesting that we regularly tell patients what we think they ought to be doing. But I think we owe it to our patients to listen, as much as we are able, from their subjective perspective for the relevance of these seemingly objective issues.

3 Beauty Treatment
The Aesthetics of the Psychoanalytic Process

Ye know on earth, and all ye need to know.

JOHN KEATS (1819)

PSYCHOANALYSTS LOVE DOING PSYCHOANALYSIS for reasons above and beyond its helpfulness to patients. While it is the responsibility of the analyst by and large to be selfless, to be there for the patient, the analyst is also inevitably and irreducibly present as a subjective being (Renik 1993). There are thus unavoidable narcissistic pleasures (and non-pleasures) for the analyst, and it is obviously essential for the analyst to be as aware as possible of what his or her stake in the process may be. One of the most intense pleasures I have experienced is awe of the beauty of the analytic process itself. Aesthetic pleasure is a highly sublimated libidinal satisfaction. The analytic process, I propose, can be understood as aesthetic in that is possesses a form—equivalent to that of artistic objects—that can be evaluated, appreciated, and enjoyed. I will discuss four intertwined components of the analytic process as aesthetic—meaning-making, love, communication, and professional craft—and I will speculate about the nature and primitive significance of the pleasures analysts derive from these elements.

Why do I even think to apply a concept such as beauty to psychoanalysis? What kind of an object or endeavor is analysis, such that it could be thought to possess a quality such as beauty? To say that analysis is both art and science is to do no more than repeat the tension in the field that others have articulated, and the concept of beauty is alive in both areas—art and science. We regard works of art as intended to be aesthetic objects, and we are not surprised to hear scientists and mathematicians speak of the beauty or elegance of their formulae or discoveries—or even of seeing the handiwork of God in the discovered scaffolding of the natural universe. Ultimately, however, beauty lies in the eye of the beholder, and how we define beauty, what we determine to be an aesthetic object, is an expression of our subjectivity. As Gilbert Rose (1980) notes:

> Science and art both create metaphors which make it possible to deal with certain things—metaphors which effect new linkages and reorder the data of experience, according a lasting reality to aspects of the world which before did not exist for us. A creative worker, whether artist or scientist, reorganizes the world in some fresh way—the artist through developing forms, the scientist through new concepts. One mode—be it artistic form or scientific concept—is not more arbitrary than the other (79).

In my view, psychoanalysis inhabits some sort of middle ground, partaking of both the artistic and the scientific.

Ogden (1994) has written about the analytic third, about the analysis as an object that is neither analysand nor analyst. It is in this sense that I think of an analysis as an object, one that results from an intensely creative process on the part of both participants. The location of the aesthetic experience is not, however, in the object itself, but rather in the meaning given to the experience of the analytic process by analyst and analysand, separately and together. Although I took an aesthetic pleasure in the process of my own personal analysis, I attribute this in part to my professional involvement with the field. Most analysands would not seek or notice aesthetic pleasure in their analyses, and I do not believe that the success of an analysis is predicated upon a conscious appreciation of this aesthetic quality. However, this appreciation of the beauty of an analysis is different from the beauty of empathy or of a good interpretation, and these latter elements are indeed sought or even craved by patients. But what I am addressing in this chapter is not primarily the work of the analysis that takes place in the mind of the patient (although my thoughts bear on this), but rather the experience of the analyst.

What is beautiful (or aesthetically pleasing) and what is gratifying for the analyst cannot be entirely separated. I would understand the aesthetic to involve a degree of sublimation that we would not ordinarily expect to find in certain instinctually or narcissistically gratifying experiences. The latter, too, would have a much closer connection to the biological than would be found in aesthetic pleasure. In other words, aesthetic pleasure takes place at a greater distance from purely bodily pleasure. In the analytic process, just as in music, painting, architecture, literature, and other fine arts, the beauty we find is in large part based on our understanding of how this object relates to other similar objects. In other words, our experience is informed by our familiarity with particular traditions and rituals. And thus, the pleasure is indeed based on a sublimation or on a symbolic act, an interpretation of the meaning of the communication between artist and observer. It is in this sense that the gratifications for the analyst (and for the patient) in the analytic process can also be understood to be aesthetic. Although their developmental roots are in the libidinal, these pleasures derive from highly symbolized and interpretive activities.

Obviously, psychoanalysis differs from the fine arts in two important respects. First, it is an entity created by a twosome formed not to make art but to relieve suffering. It might be said, though, that insofar as there is something beautiful about health and the development of a well-functioning individual, the analytic dyad's purpose is to create beauty where it may have been lacking. Perhaps the analytic process can be seen as beautiful in the sense that we find natural phenomena to be so. However, psychoanalysis, unlike a sunset, is a cultural artifact. Second, unlike most aesthetic objects, analysis is always in the process of creation, incomplete until termination. But in some respects, the analytic process is experienced in the way one does a symphony or a novel. I understand the significance of the object I contemplate—that is, any segment of an analysis—in relation to what has come before and to the fact that I anticipate that there is more to come. Any segment is a part of an ongoing narrative. And I have certain hopes about what kind of thing is to come. The difference is that what is to come does not yet exist. The unit I contemplate, however, must have been completed—for how else am I to have perceived it if it is not yet an "it"?[1] As Loewald (1975) notes: "Patient and analyst are in a sense co-authors of the play: the material and the actions of the transference neurosis gain structure and organization by the organizing work of the analyst" (280).

One of my most influential teachers in high school cautioned me that it is very difficult to write what he termed "an appreciation paper." Nonetheless, I proceeded to attempt this (an essay, as I recall, about humor in Sinclair Lewis's *Arrowsmith*) and naturally got a "C" (or some such grade) on it. Thus, it is with some trepidation that I set out to do this in regard to psychoanalysis, to try to explicate why it seems to me to be such a satisfying and ultimately beautiful process—and a process about which I have so much passion. But unlike my *Arrowsmith* paper, which discussed something almost everybody agrees is pleasurable, my understanding of the aesthetic in analysis is not limited to the positively valenced material. I mean to include in this conception the negative as well—the anger and hatred, the anxiety, enactments, and episodes of disjointedness that are a necessary part of all treatments.

Clinical Illustrations

Let me begin my attempt to define something indefinable, the beauty of the analytic process, by describing two very different patients and processes. I will begin not with an ugly process but rather with an absence of process.

A few years ago, I was asked to present a case to a senior analyst from another city. Because of issues of confidentiality, the only case I could present at the time was one that was not going terribly smoothly. The consulting analyst, in a phone conversation before the presentation, commented that I seemed to be quite aware of my own countertransference. I noticed, however, that as I spoke to him, there was a certain aspect of my experience that I could not put into words. I could only capture my feelings with something approaching a groan of complaint or distress. It was so uncharacteristic of me to be unable to put my thoughts into words that I began considering what it was about this case that prompted my feelings, for this was a patient whom I did not dislike.

In a typical hour, Eliza, a teacher, enters the office, lies down, and remains silent for a minute or two. Her anxiety manifests itself in the slight stiffness of her body even before she speaks. She begins to talk about something or other that is on her mind, always something connected with reality. The red thread is often difficult for me to find. My first intervention might be a simple reflection or clarification of Eliza's feelings; sometimes she allows that what I say is true, while at other times she simply continues with what she was saying, reporting diligently the glory of mundane detail in which she lives (as do we all). Efforts to point out the process to her, that she has ignored what I have said, may result in an irritated compliance, but in the end, she remains aggressively adherent to the reality.

I have come to believe that this attachment to reality, virtually impervious to interpretation, represents a displacement or a foreclosure of internal experience. In one sense, there has been very significant progress: Eliza knows now that what troubles her comes from her own mind, something she did not know at the start of analysis. In addition, her presenting symptoms have significantly abated. Nonetheless, I always have to struggle to get her to understand that reality is not all that it seems and that there exists an equally vital process of imagining within her mind. By the end of some hours, she does seem to glimpse this. But it is gone by the next session. Perhaps a better metaphor here than the red thread would be that of Hansel and Gretel: All the crumbs on the forest floor have been eaten, and the patient and I are lost.

Every few months, there is a session or a series of sessions in which Eliza does seem able to work in a way that I would consider analytic. But often these fruitful sessions are followed by cancellations. And again, the reality issues seem so compelling to her that she has not been able to see that there is a volitional element to these cancellations. Eliza millimeters along, and it is certainly not clear that she is truly analyzable (at least by me at this time). Her attempts to kill meaning-making, which I have interpreted, seem themselves to be impervious to interpretation.

It could well be that what I was experiencing with this patient as a process without beauty might have transformed itself into an ugly phase in a process that would later seem beautiful to me, although in this case, it did not. What was missing from the treatment were the elements I consider both beautiful and essential to the analytic process: meaning-making, a dialogue (in Spitz's [1965] sense of the term), love reinforced by evidence of ongoing growth and benefit to the patient, and a sense of working effectively with theories and techniques. Analysts have, very appropriately and necessarily, learned to expand into working with "widening-scope" patients. And I would place Eliza in this category, because of her minimal psychological mindedness. But that does not mean that many analysts do not have preferences. It is far better to be open about the pleasures we like to derive from our work than to pretend not to have any hopes along these lines.[2]

It is important to consider the element of time as well as the ratio of interpretability to imperviousness. There are episodes of dissonance and inaccessibility in all analyses, but it is when they persist over an extended time, or when there are no areas in which work is proceeding, that I might begin to think of an analytic process as unattainable. What I am describing is perhaps the absence of another aesthetic element, that of the therapeutic alliance. I am aware that other analysts might consider this absence of process to be the process, and that others might have been able to engage Eliza in a more helpful way. However, I think that I may well have been a good-enough analyst for Eliza; there may have been a way in which she was refusing to allow me to be a significant object and refusing to acknowledge this refusal. This amounted to a repudiation of an analytic process. Perhaps my limitation was that I was unable to work within her cultivation of emptiness, which amounted to an aggressive destruction of my analytic function.

Quite clearly, revealing what I like and do not like is tantamount to defining my limits as an analyst. We need to discover under what conditions we will feel adequate gratification in our work.[3] It was through analyzing my frustration and dissatisfaction with the work with Eliza that I came to realize that the intense pleasure I was experiencing with my other analytic patients was also suspect. The intensity of my pleasure with other patients, this countertransference "symptom," diminished significantly after I interpreted to myself the aesthetic aspect of the pleasure, and simultaneously, my discomfort and sense of paralysis in the hours with Eliza lessened. I took this as confirmation of the accuracy of my self-analysis and hypothesis.

Let me describe a very different hour.[4]

Dorothy, a recent college graduate, is twelve minutes late, a typical occurrence.[5] She begins by saying that she got very tired on the drive to my office and is feeling a little headachy. Then she tells of an old friend who is in town for a visit. She was very glad to hear from her, but when Dorothy mentioned to her that she is still in analysis four times a week, the friend said, "You still go?" The patient then speaks about how bad she feels about this, even though she knows why she's coming to treatment.

I comment that she does seem to be clearer than she's ever been about what she wants to accomplish here, but that it is also hard for her to hold onto this in the face of her friend's exclamation. Dorothy nods as I speak and says that it is hard for her to believe that it's okay. She goes on to say that she realizes she sets up encounters like this one in which she knows the other person will question the analysis. She wonders if she does this in order to punish herself.

I say that perhaps it might be to save herself from the pressures and uncertainties of feeling so good about herself. Dorothy replies that she hadn't thought about it in that way before, that it might be to protect herself. Basically, she says, it is hard for her to be happy about anything, to be okay with something. She brought up that in yesterday's session—she talked about looking at job listings in the classified advertisements, even though she loves her new job.

I comment that it's hard for her to stick with something when she feels other people don't understand it or have a different opinion. The patient observes that, as I was speaking, she was thinking of how her parents' opinions always prevail over her own, that her ideas aren't taken seriously and don't matter. This has happened for so long that she starts to think that maybe her parents are right, and so she doesn't stick with her own feelings. She guesses that maybe it isn't such a surprise that she acted that way with her friend. Then she pauses, turns on her side, and speaks about how tired she is, how heavy her mind feels, and that it is becoming an effort to talk. She says she could fall asleep right now, but notes that she doesn't usually get this tired at the end of a regular workday, so it must be something she's doing to herself.

I wonder aloud why this might be happening. Dorothy replies that it is because she isn't just talking about difficult things, but rather that the deeper stuff is happening "live," because she doesn't want to be here today. (This expression refers to a dichotomy that the patient and I have used to distinguish material that seems live and in color from what seems rehearsed.) She doesn't want to talk, but feels she is supposed to be talking.

I comment that Dorothy seems to feel here the way she feels with her parents, that their opinion matters and hers does not. She is assuming that I want her to talk, and it is hard for her to imagine that it would be okay with me if she did not. She first replies that it would be pointless to be here in silence, pauses, and then says that she doesn't think she could ever be comfortable doing that. She is not used to quiet; it makes her nervous.

I remind the patient of something she said the previous day: that she thought it was kind of cool that she was experiencing with me the conflicts she has elsewhere in her life. I say that because analysis is about talking, maybe it isn't a surprise that that would be the medium carrying some of the issues here, between us.

Dorothy says, "So we're dealing with something live here," and I say that I think we are. She then speaks about how she struggles not just with talking versus not talking here, but that it is hard for her to talk to me about what happens here. She yawns, pauses, then comments that that's another reason she's sleepy: she's fighting with herself because it is uncomfortable to experience things live and because she's not comfortable with not talking.

I comment that being quiet has other meanings for her, related to how chaotic and noisy her home is. She says again that quiet makes her nervous, feels threatening. There are never any uncomfortable silences at home because she always has something to say. She talks about her best friend's family, how respectful they are to each other. She comments that the friend's mother would never wake her by doing aerobics in the next room at 6:00 a.m., with the television on high volume, as her own mother does. She says that this drives her nuts, but that mother can't stand for anyone to be sleeping once she is awake. Dorothy says that quiet might be boring, but it would be nice once in a while.

I say, "I wonder if it feels here as though I'm going to intrude on you in some way if you're resting while I'm not." Dorothy answers that she'd never had that thought before, but adds immediately, "I guess so—like you're going to say, 'Dorothy, talk!'" (The last words were spoken loudly and forcefully.) She continues by saying that whenever mother is awake, it's her time, and that Dorothy always has to be doing something for her parents. She says she has been trained to feel this way, that it is very hard to break the cycle when it is still being reinforced. It's getting better lately, she adds, giving the example of having recently watched television with mother and wondering if it was really okay to be relaxing; she did not want to jinx it by asking, so she just enjoyed it while it lasted.

I comment that it's like she wants to do that here, but is scared to. She says, yeah, it is relaxing not to talk, but what if she fell asleep? She wouldn't do that; it's too weird. She describes seeing mother take a nap and wonders if she could do that, too. She then speaks about wanting to make the best of her time here, not to waste it by saying and doing nothing. If she did that, she'd be mad at herself.

I comment: "Apparently saying and doing nothing here would really be quite something." She giggles and says it would indeed be a breakthrough for her. She wonders what it would feel like, then says again that it would really be a waste of her time and mine. She pauses before remarking that she thinks this whole time thing is really important. I say, "And speaking of time . . ." She laughs. The hour is over.

Why did I experience satisfaction in this hour with Dorothy? What is the nature of the pleasure I experienced? I came to define the pleasure as aesthetic because it seemed to have to do with form, complexity, elegance—qualities supraordinate to the specific clinical content or therapeutic achievement. This aesthetic quality has two sides, one affective and the other intellectual. These categories are roughly comparable to the division between art and science and their respective gratifications. On the affective side, important elements have to do with what it means to me to create meaning and understanding where there has been confusion or even an absence of thought; with what it means to be contributing to the relief of suffering; with the significance of being involved in an effective process of communication; with joy in my own creativity; with watching the patient's mind become more complex; and with watching the patient take pleasure in her own understanding. On the intellectual side (and, naturally, there is no firm distinction between the affective and the intellectual), I think my sense of the process as aesthetic derives from the way a theory or set of theories can help me know what to say and to predict how a patient might respond. It also has to do with pleasure in one's own intellect, a kind of *Funktionslust*, that I believe all analysts experience (whether acknowledged or not).

Kris (1956) emphasized that the good analytic hour did not refer only to those characterized by positive transference. It is noteworthy that it was an art historian who articulated this idea of the goodness that I am now linking to an aesthetic quality. Kris's conception, however, places almost exclusive stress on the role of insight, and specifically, insight in the patient. I am concerned in this chapter more with the experience of the analyst than with the experience of the patient (though it is probably more difficult for the analyst to have a pleasurable experience with a patient who is not making progress, however the analyst may understand this). Those patients who demonstrate what Kris terms a "gift for analytic work" (451; e.g., Dorothy rather than Eliza) facilitate the development of what the analyst may come to experience as an aesthetic process.

It is possible for some patients to experience the process as an aesthetic object, and my guess is that this occurs most commonly in analytic candidates and other mental health professionals. (However, Dorothy's comment on how "cool" it is that all the issues she has with others are happening between us, despite her extreme fear of this very occurrence, indicates something approaching an aesthetic appreciation of the process.) While, ultimately, the success or failure of analysis is determined by what has taken place within the patient's mind, analysis is in my view a process that takes place via the analytic relationship; thus, the nature of the analyst's pleasure will inevitably have an impact on the patient. For instance, although I devoted much effort to maintaining openness and optimism in my work with Eliza, she spoke from time to time of the ways in which some of her own students tried her patience. She was able to acknowledge, briefly and in an intellectualized way, that she thought she might be frustrating me.

This acknowledgment of Eliza's suggests that what I referred to earlier as a cultivation of emptiness may have been something with larger metapsychological significance—an aesthetic of death or destructiveness. When I use the term aesthetic as a noun, I mean to invoke several concepts, psychoanalytic and ordinary—repetition compulsion, unconscious fantasy, Weltanschauung. The *American Heritage Dictionary* (2000) includes the following definition of aesthetic: "An underlying principle, a set of principles, or a view often manifested by outward appearances or style of behavior." An aesthetic can thus be understood as one's preferred mode of presentation, comportment, or display, as well as the ways in which one creates these preferred conditions through enactments with external objects. What we think of as character could also be considered a reflection of the personal aesthetic. In fact, one might think of one of the goals of analysis as replacing one aesthetic with another; and, as we know from experience, what is most difficult for patients to give up is indeed what gives them pleasure.

Returning to Eliza, might an analyst who was better able to derive pleasure from her own sadism and masochism than I am have been better able to enter Eliza's aesthetic and thus to help her? It is an unanswerable question. We know all too well that this dynamic characterizes many relationships, including mother-child, husband-wife, and analysand-analyst. Each partner becomes for the other an object of sadism rather than of love, and hatred becomes the coinage of the connection. It might be possible, I suppose, to say that such an aesthetic might yet partake of a larger aesthetic of beauty, insofar as it would fall within the capacity of psychoanalytic theory to explicate and perhaps even predict its occurrence. One might be able to say that once the cultivation of hatred can be understood, it can become beautiful (or, perhaps more accurately, sublime). But I think that to try to subsume destructiveness under beauty would minimize the fact that sadism and masochism are powerful and independent mental tendencies. Regardless of why they exist—as reflections of a destructive drive, or as byproducts of empathic failures or of having had to love a sadistic object—they do exist. In saying that the analyst should cultivate or permit an aesthetic of destructiveness only as a means to the end of helping the patient enter an aesthetic of love, I am addressing not only the aesthetics of psychoanalysis, but also its ethics.

The Aesthetics of Meaning-making: Interpretation

In the hour with Dorothy described above, the emphasis on making meaning is apparent. Through a process of clarification and interpretation, the patient and I come to understand more about her. There is an unimpeded movement in this session between present and past, transference and external life. The repetition of the past in the present and the vitality of the transference reinforces the patient's conviction about the validity of the new understanding. I do not need to explicate at any great length the various elements of psychoanalytic theory that lead to my technique: the importance of transference interpretation, the principles of ego defenses, and the use of empathy. But certainly, all of them together work elegantly and effectively to further the therapeutic process and to relieve the patient of another increment of suffering. I find an almost tangible beauty in sessions such as the one described above, typical in the work with Dorothy. No particular theoretical stance dominates here, but clearly, it is a specifically psychoanalytic theory that informs and animates the process and the result. What I cannot capture in mere words, of course, are the excitement, pleasure, and relief that Dorothy expressed.

One of the goals in an analysis is for the patient to be able to develop a more or less coherent narrative of how she came to be the way she is. I think it would be accurate, too, to say that this is one of the values that most analysts hold, that it is a good thing to be able to understand oneself in this way. It is the patient's narrative rather than the analyst's that is ultimately necessary, but one of the ways in which the patient can develop this is via the reconstructions and interpretations proposed by the analyst. The insurmountable fact of suggestibility, however, blurs the line between the narrative of the analyst and that of the patient; but as we know, the analyst's interpretations, too, are a product of both members of the dyad. Thus, my light-bulb moments in an analytic session constitute another tentative building block in the coherent image of the patient that I form in my mind and then gradually offer to the patient for her consideration, confirmation, rejection, or emendation. But to me, this is where the relationship of psychoanalysis to science also emerges, in the search for the patient's confirmatory associations, memory, or emotional resonance with the interpretation. The element of science in this is the check with reality, the experiment that takes place when the patient tries on an idea or a feeling to see if it fits.

Embedded in this goal of creating a coherent narrative are standards that are remarkably similar to the ways in which one attempts to evaluate works of art objectively. Most art criticism can be understood to address the degree of unity of a work (level of organization, formal perfection, possession of an inner logic of structure and style), the degree of complexity of a work (the largeness of scale, richness of contrasts versus repetitiveness, subtlety, or imagination), and finally, the intensity of the work (its vitality, forcefulness, beauty, and emotional type or genre) (Beardsley 1958, 462). With rather little imagination, we can apply these notions to the ways in which we critically evaluate the depth and quality of an analytic process. I would translate the criterion of unity in terms of the extent to which the transference, present and past, is understood as connected. Complexity and intensity can be applied to analysis, I think, as they have been described above. And if we consider knotty epistemological problems (e.g., narrative versus historical truth), it may make sense to evaluate the coherence and quality of the narrative more in the manner we do with a work of art than in the way we do with a newspaper article.

Psychoanalytic aesthetics appear on the surface to violate one of the oldest standards, that of the Greeks, who looked for the three unities of time, place, and actions in their dramas. (I say "appear" because in the unconscious, the need for these unities does not exist, as all things coexist at all times.) In analysis, I think we replace this with another threesome: We hope that the patient will move freely between present real life, transference, and the past. Perhaps we could think of this as the architectural structure of psychoanalysis—the rooms of the house through which we wander.[6] Another way of thinking about this is that there is always unity of time, place, and action in a patient's narrative, and it is the job of the analyst and the patient to discover it. Recall, too, that in the formation of dreams, logical considerations of representability are one of the disguising and defensive elements of the dream work. If we look at a work that straddles the border between literature and psychoanalysis, Freud's Dora (1905), we can see the struggle to create a new genre that respects the aesthetic of the unconscious in which there are no such divisions. This tension—between a traditional aesthetic or logic of narrative and the aesthetic or logic of the psyche—may account for many of the difficulties that some analysts experience in writing about their cases.

But to shift from aesthetics back to psychoanalysis, let us wonder why a coherent narrative may seem so beautiful a phenomenon to contemplate. In fact, it is not a coherent narrative that I contemplate in my vignette of Dorothy, but rather the potential for one; one could say, perhaps, that it is the movement from less to more coherence that is as much the aesthetic object as the narrative itself. And it is this that I am aiming at here, the process of making meaning as the aesthetic object rather than simply the meaning itself. In other words, it is perhaps movement in the direction of truth, rather than truth itself (which may be unknowable), that constitutes the beauty I find in the psychoanalytic process.[7] In addition, I would like to stress the aesthetic pleasure of the narrative provided by psychoanalytic theory itself. While it is not a predictor of any specific clinical event with any specific patient, psychoanalytic understanding may nonetheless include even events that surprise the analyst. As the patient and I create or discover his or her narrative, we are simultaneously discovering or contributing to the elegance of psychoanalytic theory itself.

Segal (1952) has argued that our pleasure in contemplating an aesthetic object may derive from its representation of the achievement of the depressive position, that is, from the internalization of whole as opposed to part objects. She points out that once we have attained the depressive position, what we fear is no longer an attack by persecuting objects, but rather the loss of the actual loved object and of the mental representation of that object. Repeated experiences of loss and regaining of the object lead to a more secure establishment of the object. Segal feels that aesthetic objects represent attempts to re-create lost objects, and that these lost objects are what we see and identify with as we contemplate aesthetic objects. It is the movement from chaos to order, from ugliness to beauty, from the paranoid-schizoid part object to the depressive whole object, from the death instinct to life, that explain the appeal of the aesthetic object.

Likierman (1989) argues that the aesthetic experience does not, as Segal says, emerge from the achievement of the depressive position, but rather that it is an attribute of the positive pole of the splitting characteristic of the paranoid-schizoid position: "Far from being an illusion, the ideal is an aspect of reality which is integral to any experiencing of goodness" (139). Likierman particularly emphasizes the global nature of infantile affect and experience, noting the importance of light as one very early aesthetic experience. (Note that in this chapter, I have already used metaphors of light.) In the adult world, we often associate light with understanding, and I would read Likierman's argument accordingly—as shedding light on the primacy of insight, thus supporting the views of Kris (1956).

Likierman also makes an interesting argument about the negative side of the pole: "Hunger is not the absence of food, but the presence of deprivation and pain which fill the infant to capacity and are registered at a psychic level as a present 'bad' breast" (1989, 141). I would see this as consistent with Kernberg's (1976, 1992) schema of early development. We could postulate that the positively valenced units of object-affect-self experience would have an aesthetic quality. The bodily ego is so prepared to receive these experiences with enjoyment that it is almost as if light (as well as nourishment and other physical comforts) might be intrinsically beautiful. I would maintain, however, that the aesthetic quality is in the experiencing and the meaning rather than in the object itself. Constitutional differences may influence the degree to which one develops an aesthetic sense. That adults find aesthetic qualities in aggression and destructiveness may suggest that we have all needed to learn to cultivate that which we originally had to learn to tolerate—pain and unpleasure.

Light, however, is sometimes illuminating and sometimes blinding. Let me take up here my earlier point about my ideas of aesthetics not being limited to what is facile or "pretty." Although it is certainly not pleasant to be the target of a patient's rage, I find a beauty in the process of containing and perhaps metabolizing these feelings. There is also a way of conceiving of these episodes as parts of a whole rather than as freestanding, complete in and of themselves. In contrast to the conclusions reached by many of the speakers who addressed the question of the modes of therapeutic change and good, bad, and ugly hours at a recent conference,[8] it is my sense that even certain ugly or bad hours can partake of the beauty of psychoanalysis in that they are a part of a larger whole. (Earlier, I noted this possibility in regard to Eliza.) Experiences of satisfaction are defined not simply by their tension, but also by the unit of tension and release of tension. When what has misfired can be righted, there will come into being exactly the movement from paranoid-schizoid to depressive that Segal (1952) describes as constituting the aesthetic.

Naturally, there may be a defensive quality to my thinking here, or this may be my way of seeking to transform the paranoid-schizoid fragment into the depressive whole—for the patient and for me.[9] As we know, the units of meaning in analysis do not occur in neat, forty-five-minute segments. Rather, there are different strands of various themes in each session, and it is up to patient and analyst to create the frames, to determine which elements belong together as a unit. The analytic pair is delineating the contours of the portrait even as it is being painted, or the movements of the symphony even as it is being performed. It is a miraculous opus, for its organization and key can be revised retroactively and with almost infinite variations. Dissonant chords or even entire movements need to be understood in relation to the whole.

There is beauty in the violence of a volcano's eruption as long as one observes it from a position of safety; being able to keep the "as-if" quality present even during the intensity of the moment, when it is all too real to the patient, allows the analyst this safety of distance. The patient's growth and his or her creation of the new necessarily entail the destruction of old adaptations. This makes destruction a necessary component of the psychoanalytic process—and the valuing of this destruction a necessary component of an aesthetic appreciation of that process. The therapeutic alliance and the patient's observing ego provide the position of safety. It should also be stressed that not all aggression is hostile (Parens 1979).

The Aesthetics of Communication and the Therapeutic Alliance

The aesthetics of communication—the *sine qua non* of psychoanalysis—can be understood in at least two ways. First, there are the ways in which the material that is communicated in analysis and the manner of its communication resemble artistic communication. Beres (1957) points out the similarities between communication in art and communication in psychoanalysis:

> The themes which appear in the analytic session are those of the mythmakers and poets: of birth, death, love, hate, incest, sex, perversion, parricide, matricide, destruction, violence, castration, hunger, greed, jealousy, ambition, dependence. They are themes of the forbidden, the unattainable, the repressed—and the techniques of the artist are required to present them to consciousness, even in their disguised forms. In the artistic act and in the analytic situation, the forbidden and the repressed are re-created (415).

Although his article focuses primarily on the experience of the patient, Beres speaks as well of the requirement of the analyst to participate more than passively in the creative process—through receptivity to the patient's unconscious communications, through the ability to form creative thoughts of his or her own while hearing this material, and through the willingness and ability to respect the patient's individuality. This latter, Beres says, derives from the analyst's success at "having lived through a creative experience in his own analysis" (419).

Beres makes another important point (1957, 420) about the ways in which the psychoanalytic process resembles a work of art, such as in the need for a suspension of disbelief. We immerse ourselves in fiction or drama by pretending that it is real, but at the same time preserving the understanding that this is not really happening. It is in this way that the experience can be cathartic or therapeutic, because we know we can come back from these other emotions even as they are evoked in us; this is the safe distance from the erupting volcano. Similarly, both analysts and patients depend on this "as-if" quality in the therapeutic relationship. As analysts, we experience empathy for our patients, feel their pains and pleasures as though they were ours, yet we know with confidence that we will return to our own minds. And we depend on our analysands to be able to experience the transference intensely, but also in an "as-if" fashion. Finally, Beres emphasizes that unlike the situation of works of art—in which the unconscious material remains unarticulated—it is the goal of psychoanalysis to bring as much of the unconscious as possible into the realm of the conscious world of language (421).

The second way in which the subject of communication can be understood is according to its developmental significance for both patient and analyst. Likierman (1989) and Mitrani (1998) have addressed the ways in which the experience of beauty is an integral part of infantile life. Mitrani, in particular, writes of the mother's responsibility to allow her child to find her beautiful and indeed awesome. (This is a primitive form of what Kohut [1971] described as the child's necessary idealization of the parents.) Neither Likierman nor Mitrani makes reference to Spitz's (1965) notion of "the dialogue," a concept closely related to their arguments and to mine. Spitz describes "the dialogue" as follows:

> By far the most important factor in enabling the child to build gradually a coherent ideational image of his world derives from the reciprocity between mother and child. . . . The dialogue is the sequential action-reaction-action cycle within the framework of mother-child relations. This very special form of interaction creates for the baby a unique world of his own, with its specific emotional climate. It is this action-reaction-action cycle that enables the baby to transform step by step meaningless stimuli into meaningful signals (42).

The dialogue is not of neutral emotional valence; rather, it is exactly what Likierman describes as beautiful, insofar as it contributes to the creation of coherence, light, and understanding. It is thus an aesthetic experience. In my view, this is the second crucial feature of communication in psychoanalysis that justifies thinking of it as an aesthetic process. Regardless of the content of the communication, whether at any given moment there will be an insight, growth, or relief for the patient, the very fact that responsive communication exists qualifies it as a version of the dialogue, reminiscent for both participants of a well-working mother—infant dyad. The dialogue in analysis can be thought of as a corrective emotional experience, in the best sense of the term—not as a contrived cure-all, but rather as an outgrowth of a good-enough analyst's listening and responsiveness; perhaps it is not inappropriate to describe psychoanalysis as a treatment by beauty.

The Aesthetics of Love

Whether or not we analysts can be said to love our patients in the ordinary sense of the word, our desire to help, to relieve suffering, to promote understanding, and to enhance patients' ability to pursue happiness all reflect some form of love. Just as analysts cannot (and should not, in my view) be neutral in this regard, so, too, can this non-neutrality be understood in larger terms. Lear (1998) has argued that the human mind has been structured by love, by a good-enough environment. While love certainly can signify closeness and connection, in another sense, love leads to greater differentiation and complexity. In other words, it is the good-enough nature of the earth that permitted humans to evolve from single-celled creatures, and it is the same force of good-enoughness that was and is the midwife of the mind. In the same sense that light (and later, understanding) can be thought of as possessing an aesthetic quality, so too, I believe, can love.

To return to my patient Dorothy: Dorothy begins a Monday session by describing an experience she had over the weekend. She is thinking about something that came up in a session the previous week, her restlessness and tendency to want to move on to something else in her school and work, asking herself what was behind this feeling. She said: "It just came to me, it was weird. I just kind of felt like my head cleared. Wow! When I say it to you, it won't sound like a revelation [spoken shyly], but I came to it myself. What I was thinking—the thing that was so cool was that it really hit my feelings, I knew that was how I felt—I think when I look for something else, it gives me a guarantee that I won't be stuck somewhere. That's what I'm afraid of, that I'll be stuck." And she continues to explore this fruitfully.

The very fact that Dorothy was describing with textbook clarity what an accurate interpretation should feel like provided me with aesthetic pleasure (in the sense of being an example of the elegance of this aspect of psychoanalytic theory). However, what caused me to smile from my seat behind her was the fact that she had achieved this on her own, that this represented a very significant piece of self-analytic work. Dorothy came to analysis with a natural inquisitiveness, but she had been unable to utilize it in regard to herself for two reasons. First, she was constantly overwhelmed by her feelings and did not know where to begin; second, she had a sense that she was not important enough to spend time understanding herself, that her needs always came last. In this vignette, I saw that she had been able to internalize my interest in her, a reflection of my love, caring, and my view that she was worthwhile. This resulted in greater differentiation in Dorothy's mind, a greater capacity to make meaning, and greater individuation born out of the connection with me.

Psychoanalysis, to me, is the opposite of soul murder (Shengold 1991), and ultimately, it is an expression of love. I see its greatest beauty in just this, its potential to generate soul, to create, to give life to the mind. In my view, this is closely related to the way in which Donnel Stern asserts that what turns analysts on is the potential for freedom they sense in their patients (Stern 1999). The concept of freedom is, for me, embedded in the notion of giving life. And this brings me back to Segal's (1952) argument: "Re-stated in terms of instincts, ugliness—destruction—is the expression of the death instinct; beauty—the desire to unite into rhythms and wholes, is that of the life instinct. The achievement of the artist [and, I would add, the analyst] is in giving the fullest expression to the conflict and the union between those two" (505). My emphasis is not only on the altruism of the analyst, his or her vicarious pleasure for the patient, but also on the aggressive, libidinal, and narcissistic satisfactions the process provides for the analyst—on the pleasures and beauty of loving one's patients within the bounds of this peculiar and wonderful discipline of psychoanalysis. This, to me, is where the work of analysis most resembles the experience of parenthood, of loving, holding, admiring, differentiating, and letting go. Parents and analysts hate their children and patients, too, but when parents and analysts are good enough, this hatred does not impinge upon the central task of generating or celebrating their children's and patients' souls. When parents do not let their children individuate, for example, or when analysts do not reflect on and manage any excessive enjoyment of power over their patients, they are falling short of fulfilling their roles in an ethical manner.

The Aesthetics of Professional Craft

Art is created or performed for an audience, and we analysts perform not only for the patient, but also for the internalized audience of our peers, mentors, students, and personal analysts. Through our analytic and other clinical training, we have learned which kinds of interventions evoke applause. We have both applauded and frowned upon our colleagues; we have learned to be humble about our work (if we are wise); we have figured out that our own instincts with patients are generally good enough (at the very least). Consensual validation from our peers has helped us develop the confidence that we know how to perform in a particular genre, that we know how to play by the rules. Even in the isolation of our offices, we carry a sense of twinship and camaraderie with other professionals; we feel ourselves a part of a community of like-minded people who take pleasure in certain things and commiserate about others.

I would like to address the intervention in the longer vignette described above in which I wondered whether Dorothy feared that I would intrude on her if she was resting when I was not. I like this interpretation, and I think it was effective. But as to the particular mixture of all the elements operative at that moment, I cannot say, for instance, exactly why I decided to draw the patient's attention to the transference. Like the performance art of great cuisine, psychoanalysis is also a disappearing act that is savored, simultaneously vanishing even as it becomes a permanent part of each participant. And unlike the performance art of a symphony, in which the number and types of instruments can be specified, the art of interpretation can never be practiced under anything remotely approaching controlled conditions. (I am thinking of instruments here not as analysts often speak of themselves as the analytic instrument, but rather as the various elements that can be combined in order to form an interpretation.) To carry the music metaphor a bit further, one could think about the oscillation between major and minor, the tones, percussive episodes, slow and fast movements, solos, duets, choruses, and so forth by which an analysis could be characterized.

Do I choose to use the form of a statement or a question? What is the mix of affect, drama, humor, seriousness, and logic in my language? When do I decide to be playful, as I did at the end of the session described earlier? To what extent do I decide to use the patient's idioms? And what tones and cadences will my voice assume when I speak? Will I be matter-of-fact? Gentle? Firm? When do I focus on transference and when on extratransference material? And, perhaps above all, when do I decide to try to communicate my understanding to the patient?

I do not mean to suggest that my work is unusual in these respects; rather, I am offering this as an example of the potentially aesthetic judgments that analysts make all the time—and of the aesthetic pleasure they may experience as a result of those judgments. I bring up these issues, familiar to every analyst, in order to stress the degree of creativity and artistry embedded in each interpretation. Loewald (1960) addresses this point: "Language, in its most specific function in analysis, as interpretation, is thus a creative act similar to that in poetry, where language is found for phenomena, contexts, connexions, experiences not previously known and speakable" (26). At every point of speaking, an analyst must consider what will be digestible, palatable, or even pleasing to the patient. A remark that is too bitter may well be rejected, while a spoonful of sugar, on the other hand. . . . And just as for the chef, the goal for the analyst is to be familiar enough with a variety of recipes and genres so as to be unimpeded by those tools while in the act of cooking.[10]

Although both patient and analyst consume the same material, taste buds are different, so the experience is different. In fact, perhaps part of what goes into the recipe for an interpretation is the analyst's having the patient in her mind to the degree of being able to imagine which flavors and textures will be palatable and digestible at that particular moment. We choose sweet or salty, bitter or tangy, garlic, peppermint, or even jalapeño for our audience of one. Just as a ballerina must manage to achieve self-expression within the bounds of choreography and music not of her own composition, so, too, do we analysts do this in our listening, our attention to our inner responses, and our utilization of both inner and outer as we craft our utterances. And let us not neglect to acknowledge the aggression inherent in and necessary to these activities (Raphling 1992), as well as the role of the analyst's fantasies of creation (as I described in chapter 1).

What was most striking—and aesthetic in quality—to me about this hour with Dorothy was the paradox about the meaning to the patient of talking and not talking. To be able comfortably to remain silent would represent simultaneously both a resistance and a developmental achievement for Dorothy. This kind of tension or ambiguity—a not uncommon characteristic of psychoanalytic work[11]—I experienced as both unsettling and awe inspiring. To me, this was like the story of the lady and the tiger, Manet's *Bar at the Folies Bergère*, or an Escher drawing. It was unsettling because I did not know what to do with it, and also awe-inspiring because I did not know what to do with it. Seeking the truth—what was the meaning of not speaking?—I was forced to acknowledge that there was no single meaning here.

Just as there are tensions that animate works of art, I felt as though I was contemplating the tension that makes up the mind itself. That there are no negatives in the unconscious, that the mind operates according to the principle of multiple function—these are commonplace observations for an analyst. To consider such an irresolvable conundrum is to contemplate the ultimate source of the aesthetic: the complexity and elegance of the mind itself, its mechanisms and creativity and unpredictability. The profound satisfaction of helping, of making meaning, of contributing to another person's capacity to find peace and self-knowledge—in sum, the privilege of being able to express and enact one's values in one's work—these are, to me, the analyst's unavoidable gratifications, the beauty in the sometimes elusive and painful truths of psychoanalysis and in the structure of the psychoanalytic process.

Notes

1. This is, in a sense, the same argument Renik (1993) makes about countertransference, that action necessarily precedes awareness.

2. There is a distinction between the analyst's attempting to shape a treatment in order to fulfill certain preferences and the analyst's appreciating when an analysis evolves in such a way as to satisfy those preferences. The first I would consider a potential countertransference pitfall. However, it may be impossible and even undesirable for the analyst entirely to avoid trying to shape the analysis. The values

(honesty, desire to relieve suffering, respect) and aesthetics of the analyst are essential to the treatment's potential helpfulness.

3. These conditions will differ with each analyst and patient dyad. With some patients, not being yelled at is sufficient. Optimally, the analyst will accurately assess the patient's capabilities. But in this chapter, I am addressing not whether we can tolerate drinking Manischewitz, but whether we would prefer Chateau d'Yquem. I am also not suggesting that the latter would be as delectable if we drank it with every meal.

4. In that I have greatly abridged the patient's associations, this vignette is skewed in emphasizing my interventions as opposed to my long silences.

5. Perhaps it should be said that Dorothy's sessions were not good hours but good half-hours. Her lateness and cancellations contrasted starkly with Eliza's in that they were eminently analyzable. While they obviously had aggressive content, they did not represent an attack on the very process of meaning-making.

6. We could also consider the phases of analysis (beginning, middle, termination, post-termination) as part of an architecture. And id, ego, superego—the elements of the structural theory—provide a mental architecture in which we can locate different functions and tendencies.

7. I use *truth* here in the sense of *narrative truth*.

8. "Analytic Hours: The Good, the Bad, and the Ugly," Psychoanalytic Electronic Publishing CD-ROM Conference, New York, February 1999.

9. All clinicians find their own ways of tolerating what they find unpleasant about their work, and this is my way.

10. At least, this is how *I* cook. And I must admit, as well, that I am virtually unable to use a recipe without changing something in it in order to improve it and make it my own.

11. I can think of another patient with whom this kind of paradox took on a most painful affective cast. This young artist desperately needed for me to understand her, but her autonomy and boundaries had been so violated that my every attempt to communicate understanding felt like another violation. It was as though she had been sunburned, and my application of what I meant to be a soothing balm felt to her like sandpaper.

To Have and to Hold
On the Experience of Having an Other

4

TO CAPTURE A SENSE OF WHAT IT MEANS to have an Other is elusive, to say the least. Like Kohut's (1977) profound comparison of empathy to oxygen, Other-having has, so far, been most readily defined by the effects of object loss. There is a vast literature on the subject of object loss, the opposite of Other-having. But what is the metapsychological/theoretical, as well as the subjective, significance of such expressions as "I have a child," "I have a husband," or "my analyst," "my patient"? These common colloquial usages, which we all understand without difficulty, can be taken to refer not only to the world of external reality, but also—very accurately, I would suggest—to the internal world of objects. There is value in trying to link our psychoanalytic metapsychology with common ways of speaking and thinking; our common speech carries profound truths.

The mechanism by which one comes to have an object depends on initial, actual interactions with real Others.[1] Solidification of the sense of having an Other and subsequent relationships with the external Other are then facilitated by that internalized mental representation and by the represented relationship with that object. I hope that "Other" imparts a more humane, holistic, and experience near view than "object," the way many in our field refer to the real people in our patients' lives. A note on terminology: I will use Other to refer to the conscious or preconscious sense of the external person and object to refer to the mental representation of that person. I will also use object in such stock phrases as object loss and object relations, as other writers have traditionally done. However, it is often unclear in the analytic literature whether object refers to an actual person or to a mental representation or to both; consider, for instance, the expressions object loss, object permanence, object representation, and object relations. The term is variously used and I do not presume to settle any definitional issues.

A Definition of Other-having

"To have and to hold" is a phrase best known from the ritual words of the traditional marriage ceremony, and it is to make the connection to marriage (as well as to Winnicott) that I have selected this as the title for this chapter on the subject of having. Although lay persons think of having and holding in connection with weddings, Black's *Law Dictionary* (1990) tells us something different about the source of these words—that they refer to the conveyance of property in deeds. Known as the *habendum clause*, these words usually follow "the granting part of a deed, which defines the extent of ownership in the thing granted to be held and enjoyed by the grantee" (710).

For my purposes, the definition given for the single word *habere*, from the Latin *to have*, is intriguing: "In the civil law, to have. Sometimes distinguished from *tenere* (to hold), and *possidere* (to possess); *habere* referring to the right, *tenere* to the fact, and *possidere* to both" (1990, 710). This reminds us that marriages used to be contracts (and perhaps still are in some parts of the world) about the conveyance of a piece of property, a woman, from father to husband, the property owners. And although we have come to use the word "having" casually, it is indeed about possession, ownership, and the power to use that which one possesses. (It is interesting, too, that we speak about the feeling of "losing one's mind," but not nearly as readily about the feeling of "having one's own mind.")

This has implications for the therapeutic situation, as well as for the understanding of development. The feeling of having important Others is a crucial component of healthy development; it depends on having objects in one's mind and holding them—that is, having the freedom to use them productively in fantasy and playfully in reality. This having of the external Other and the internal object is a vital component of psychoanalysis as well, for this may be the patient's first opportunity for possession without bounds set by the Other's excessive narcissistic needs.

The meaning of "having" for adults is clearly related to the desire to have and to archaic experiences of having. The initial sense of object-having is related to the establishment of object permanence, that is, to the sense of Others and things continuing to exist while they are physically absent; more mature object-having, though, comes into being with the achievement of object constancy. Infants, of course, do not initially seek and covet in the way adults do (although one may certainly wonder—from the perspective either of drive or of object relations theory—whether there is some inborn, hardwired striving to "have" either need satisfaction or Others themselves; if the infant, for example, is pre-wired to attach to Others, this sense of attachment could be experienced as "having"[2]). I do not want to address this at length, because others have dealt extensively with the questions of need, desire, wish, envy, and greed; however, I will outline some of the ways these issues may intersect with my own topic. I would also like to point out that, if we have any doubts about the significance of possessiveness in development, we need only remember that the word "mine" is one of the earliest lexical achievements, preceding the use of "I."[3] The sense of having (the absence of which is not having—e.g., wanting, needing, or wishing) may go hand in hand with the sense of being, and may be articulated at an even earlier point. Later in development, of course, comes the crisis of having/not having par excellence: the Oedipal situation.

This is a theory not only of object relations in the most technical sense—that is, of relations between internalized object representations—but also of how actual relationships exist between persons. Perhaps the knottiest issue is the relationship of the fantasy or feeling of having to the actual person/Other in the real world. There is also the interesting question of whether Other-having, of the variety I am considering, can occur in the absence of the willingness to give oneself to the Other: "Who giveth this woman . . .?" Marriage, after all, involves a willingness not only to be given or had, but also to give oneself. Lacan's (1958) distinction between need, demand, and desire is relevant here. He uses "need" to refer to the biological requirement, "demand" to refer to the insistence on recognition that accompanies need (recall here Kohut's [1977] dictum that infants do not just need food—they need empathically modulated food-giving), and "desire" to refer to that which can never be satisfied, the quotient that always remains unfulfilled. Boris (1990) puts this succinctly: "For the baby to develop it is not enough for him to be gratified: he must also know that he is being gratified. This knowledge is a necessary precursor of knowing that there is a person there who is providing the gratification" (128–29). Winnicott (1951), too, when he says that there is no such thing as a baby, acknowledges the parallel between actual time-space relationships and the developing structure of the mind.

Other-having, as I am defining it, is closely related to the concept of object constancy. Object constancy is usually thought of in a positive sense—that is, as a productive and necessary building block of mental structure (Fraiberg 1969); however, we know that it is often a sadistic or excessively ambivalent Other that is internalized. Even when a "good-enough" Other is available, there must inevitably be aspects of badness present in the internalization. Perhaps it makes sense to conceptualize "good enough" as including elements that are "bad but not too bad." This bad-but-not-too-bad element in object constancy leads to the harsh introjects, the internal persecutors or punitive superego functions, that constitute the bread and butter of psychoanalytic work. Internalized objects can be persecuting, harsh, and antilibidinal, as Klein, Fairbairn, and Kernberg have eloquently described.

But Other-having, as I am attempting to define it, derives from the positively valenced internalized object. It results from the confident expectation (Benedek 1938) in time-space reality and later in mental life that one is free to take and use the good enough Other. Lear (1998) offers a compelling argument that it is love that is responsible for the very structuring of the mind, that we require a good-enough world in order to become human. I concur with Lear, and believe that it would not be possible to survive beyond infancy if relying solely or even primarily on persecutory internal objects. As we know from work with severely abused children, who persist in idealizing their abusers, survival in such environments depends upon denial and disavowal of the severity and inevitability of the trauma suffered. To the extent that our actual Others and internalized objects are not just "bad but not too bad," but rather are actually traumatogenic, we need to engage in some level of denial of their propensity to inflict trauma in order to survive. In other words, nobody *can* expect the Spanish Inquisition, even when we know it is likely to occur.

Having: Its Roots in Fantasy and Reality

The relationship between having in the dimension of reality (that is to say, in time-space) and having in the dimension of the mind is a complex one. There is obviously a real correspondence between the actual Other in time-space and the mental representation of that Other. As Boris (1990) notes: "Part of the 'goodness' of supplies may be actual and may consist in the care the mother or Other is able to offer" (138). But as many have emphasized, the situation is more complicated than a simple one-to-one correspondence with reality, for one can internalize an aspect of reality that is imagined rather than actual (see, for instance, Schafer 1968, 9).

The prototype of giving, of course, is the nursing situation, in which, if our understanding of early experience is correct, the infant does not distinguish the breast as something that does not belong to him or her. If the mother cannot allow the baby to have the illusion that the breast belongs to him or her, then the infant will experience excessive frustration. The theory of infantile hallucinations (and of dreams as wish fulfillments) explains the mind's attempt to have for the self what, in fact, is lacking, to restore that which one does not have. The breast is a metaphor for the larger task of ordinarily devoted parents to give of themselves. The word "devote," in fact, means the giving up or applying of oneself to something. Perhaps devotion can be understood to satisfy the demand (in the Lacanian sense) for recognition. It should also be noted that there can be no having without the Other's capacity for knowing—for perceiving and empathizing with the child in a way that is adequately free of conflict, projection, and narcissism.

True object-having depends on a sense of security in the possession—that is, on the freedom to hold (not in the Winnicottian sense)—and therein lies the relation of giving to having. What is vital here is the feeling that one has taken something that has been freely offered, as opposed to having stolen something that is made available grudgingly or not at all. If a bad, persecuting breast is all that is "offered," will the baby take it in? Don't the best theories about the earliest months of life suggest that the infant by and large rejects or tries to eliminate what is unpleasant? But beggars cannot be choosers, and it is clear that infants have to love the one they're with, even if that requires them to alter their sense of need and satisfaction—they learn to obtain gratification from the bad stuff that is the stuff of their lives. This is the essence of Berliner's (1940) understanding of masochism.

But, to return to the issue of having, it is not clear that the infant will truly have this need-satisfying but simultaneously non-demand-gratifying Other. Theoretically, it is possible that the infant may only truly be able to have a good Other, in the sense that I am delineating the concept of having (again, in the same sense that Lear has described the centrality of love). I am dichotomizing here for the sake of clarity. Naturally, few Others in the real world are either entirely good or entirely bad. I prefer not to speak of good-enough Others here, however, because I want to emphasize that it is the good aspects of an Other that result in a sense of having.

Two important components of the capacity for empathy in the parents are the willingness and ability to "have" the baby—that is to say, to have in their minds an internalized image of the baby that is fairly accurate.[4]

Successful development depends on this having and on devotion. The willingness to give oneself to be internalized, owned, and used by the child may be one of the most important tasks of holding in the Winnicottian sense. Only a very precarious sense of having can be attained in the absence of the Other's desire and ability to give. The characteristics of infants (and patients) are obviously relevant here, for some are needier than others, and some may be born with less capacity to use even good-enough psychological provisions. Perhaps "dandelion children" (Anthony 1990) have the capacity to develop a sense of having even under circumstances in which they have to scrounge for supplies, just as this flower can thrive even in a field of rocks.[5]

But one cannot securely have and hold that which one has gotten only by begging, borrowing, or stealing—and which may be taken back. (One of the injuries of the Oedipal period is the child's discovery of his or her non-possession not only of the desired person but also of the previously presumed knowledge.) The outlook is not always sunny, as we know too well. When a child is traumatized by environmental failures, he or she may be overwhelmed by negative affects, which in turn are not contained and metabolized by the Other. An insecure or avoidant attachment pattern will develop, and the child's capacity to use Others may be permanently impaired. When patients with this kind of history come to analysis, we see them struggle to manage the negative affects, to learn to rely on the analyst as a new and usable Other, and to develop a constant and adequately positive representation of the analyst and of the self.

What is it, precisely, that the infant comes to have and to hold? As Novey (1958) commented: "We have no difficulty in the biological sphere in perceiving that ingested food undergoes various biochemical and physical processes before becoming an intrinsic part of the organism, but we seem to have much greater difficulty in perceiving of an equivalent process in the psychic sphere" (73).

Sometimes objects are digested, such as in the mourning process, when we take in aspects of the lost Other and integrate those characteristics into our functioning. But we also have the object as a more or less whole image in our heads, in a way that is perhaps akin to the manner in which transitional objects are used. They are simultaneously both real Others and fantasy objects. While I would not want to minimize the importance of fantasy, I believe, along with Stern (1985), that the infant initially experiences reality relatively accurately. The capacity to fantasize, to imagine something other than what is, is a developmental achievement that results from the laying down of memories and the gradual entry into the world of language and symbols. With increasing age and sophistication of imagination, that which the growing child internalizes, or has, comes to consist more and more of fantasy. However, it seems to me that in the non-psychotic, the connection to actual Others never entirely vanishes; virtually every time we and our adult patients fall prey to transferences and other fantasies about Others, there is still a piece of reality in the Other on which the fantasy is based.

It is the taking in of new thought, affect, perception, or experience—in whatever admixture of reality and fantasy—that is the building block of having. Novey (1958) points out the connection between the concept of mental representation and the concept of apperception. Apperception, we recall, refers not to the actual sensation received in the organism, but involves an interpretation that is influenced by previous experiences—and also, I would argue, by the individual's participation in the existing web of language that both facilitates and limits the possibility of meaning. Blatt (1974) notes, in a discussion of Piaget, that "representation is a union of a 'signifier' with a 'signified'" (132). Although they derive from the real relationship with the mother and from the mother's existence in time-space, what we are talking about here are mental representations—shadows, ghosts, after-images of the Other—or, from the opposite perspective, creations of the individual's mind made from subjective experiences. As Boris (1990) puts it: "Identification is, of course, a fantasy given substance by mimetic activity" (127).

Just as the mother needs to allow her baby to play with her body and its accoutrements, to pull at her earrings, to put fingers in her mouth, so does the mother need to allow the baby freedom to have the illusion of owning her mind. This act of permitting oneself to be played with or used contributes to the feeling of ownership, to the sense for the infant that the external Other is subjective as well as objective (real in time-space). In the clinical situation, allowing oneself to be experienced in the transference according to the patient's needs is comparable to this parental function. Smith (2000) comments that "patients own their object representation of the analyst, and are under no obligation to modify it" (114). Prince (1974) notes that it requires courage to allow oneself to be used in this way. I would add that it takes patience—and that it also requires respect for the patient's vulnerability.

As Saul and Warner (1967) point out: "To have and to hold the love of the parents is the most important single goal of the young child's life. This same need is the core of the transference. It must be fully recognized by the patient and the analyst must be aware of its potential for damage"(538). And even when reality testing is intact, the overlap between the subjective object and the objective Other will inevitably be inexact.[6]

Thus, the relationship between reality and the mental representation is enormously complex for both infant and analysand. Kernberg (Skolnick and Scharff 1998) believes that "all internalizations are dyadic internalizations" (19). One of the cornerstones of his metapsychology is that units of internalization consisting of object, affect, and self create mental structure. To integrate this into my line of argument, then, it may be that it is not, strictly speaking, the Other that is internalized, but rather the dialogue between infant and Other (Spitz 1965).

Another way of thinking about this would be to say that giving and having are mediated first through action (including expression of affects, as Stern [1985] has so vividly described), and then through language and other symbols. But, to return to Kernberg's terminology, I am positing that it is solely the positively valenced units of object-affect-self experience—and the willingness of the parents to be used freely—that result in a sense of having for the infant. As Emde (1991) notes:

> Infant behavior has shown us that positive emotions are separately organized from negative emotions. Moreover, positive emotions are crucial for adaptation; they provide significant incentives for learning, communication, and development. For the infant and for the caregiver positive emotions are rewarding and have motivational effects that are independent of "relief" or the discharge of negative emotions (24–25).

Coates (1998) addresses the role of the parents' positive affect in her writing about the development of the child's capacity to understand the existence of mental states and intentionality in the self and the Other. This capacity, she says, does not mature until the sixth year (121). In the absence of understanding that a negative mood represents only a temporary state, the child is "simply stuck with the reality of a mother saying that he or she is a bad kid; the kid's inability to take a perspective on the attribution means that it is experienced as simply true" (120). Therefore, the child internalizes a parent's negativity as a negative sense of self.

A Philosophical View of Development

By focusing on the positive, on the potential for growth in Other-having, I am writing (and I hope not naively so) more in the romantic than in the classic paradigm of psychoanalytic thought. Strenger (1989) has outlined these opposing and often intermixed positions. Here is his summary of the distinctions between the two views:

> Psychoanalysis is characterized by a tension to be found in intellectual history at least since the eighteenth century. The classic vision of man is that of distrust of the idiosyncratic and subjective and the emphasis on the need for objectivity and rationality. In psychoanalysis this is reflected in the attitude of benevolent suspicion which seeks the traces of the pleasure principle in order to allow maturation. . . . The romantic vision sees man as essentially striving for full selfhood, and mental suffering is the result of the thwarting influence of the environment (608–9).

As I have written elsewhere (Levine 2001b), Lear's (1998) rereading of Freud throws into question the way Strenger defined his categories. Nonetheless, there are clearly two different ways of looking at humankind: one stresses the centrality of love, and the other emphasizes aggression as the default position of humankind.

By proposing that Other-having be considered to take place only in the context of the positive, growth-enhancing internalized object, I am questioning whether one really can be said to possess—that is, to have power over—a predominantly negative mental representation. Perhaps this raises the question of the extent to which all such negative internalizations should properly be thought of as identifications with an aggressor. I am not, of course, arguing that negative mental representations have no power within the self, but rather that they do not create the sense of having and holding, possessing/using/enjoying, that is a vital component of healthy development.

Having an Analyst

Despite the tendency among many analysts to think of the analytic relationship as akin to the mother-child dyad, there has also been some reluctance in our field to use this analogy. Perhaps some analysts feel that the metaphor threatens to become reified. The most common objection to the mother-child metaphor is that in adult analysis, regression is a problematic concept—it is not a literal occurrence, and it does not involve all aspects of the patient's personality and functioning. As Grunes (1984) noted:

> Basically the therapeutic object relationship consists of a situation of primal intimacy between patient and analyst which contains both an illusional (transference) and real aspect. The intimacy involves a special type of empathic permeability of boundaries between analyst and patient, which varies from an advanced, symbolic-creative level to a more primitive level of sensory, motor and somatopsychic sensations and imagery. There are

> many compelling analogies to the parent-child relationship. However, the similarities can lead us astray. For we are dealing with complex condensations, not only of child and adult, but of pathologically inflamed and updated forms of childhood developmental need. For these reasons alone the therapeutic object relationship, though similar, is radically different from the parent-child relation (131).

What I find fascinating about Grunes's description of the therapeutic object relationship in psychoanalysis is that is would also seem to capture something of the character of a marriage. Marriages, too, encourage and tolerate regressions as well as advanced levels of play, a certain permeability of boundaries, and an admixture of illusion and reality in the way one sees one's spouse. While we cannot choose our parents, we do choose our spouses—and we also choose our analysts. Within the parent-child metaphor, however, it should also be noted that parents do not choose their children. Adoption may present an interesting analogy for psychoanalysis because of the active element of choice that exists, even if an analyst only "chooses" negatively, by declining to work with a particular patient. It may also be an apt analogy in that choosing a child may give parents the illusion that they can know what they are getting into; any experienced clinician, however, knows that even the most careful and thorough initial assessment cannot prepare him or her for everything the patient will bring into the treatment.

The following vignette demonstrates the beginning of the expression of the issue of having in the therapeutic relationship. I see this young woman as a dandelion child, but as one who, at the time of this encounter, was so insecure that it did not feel to her as though she truly owned or could utilize what she in fact possessed.

Clinical Illustration

An intelligent and sensitive woman of twenty-four, the patient had been brought up in a home in which she had somehow felt both suffocated and ignored. She was paralyzed by self-doubt about her ability in her chosen field. The material I will describe, in which she talked about her struggle to achieve a generative sense of having, took place after a pivotal moment in the analysis. I had had to end a session just as the patient was speaking of the pain she felt that no one wanted her; I did this with gentle humor about the inopportuneness of the timing of the ending, and the patient—and then I—burst into laughter. Later that day, she had an experience that demonstrated how she had taken me (or the interaction between us) into her mind in a way that she could use productively; in a situation with colleagues that would previously have led her into self-recrimination, a downward spiraling mood, and plummeting self-esteem, she had experienced a surge in self-confidence, along with a certain tolerance and empathy for herself. I believe that the mutative elements in this exchange were, first, my "having" the patient in a way that led to my knowing how she might experience the ending of the session at that moment, and second, my positive feelings for her and the warmth that animated our shared laughter.

In the following session from later that week, the patient talked about liking to do things on her own—to struggle, and as a result to achieve a sense of accomplishment. This, no doubt, is partially defensive, as she had had no choice as a child but to do things independently. Nonetheless, she contrasted herself with a friend who was phobic about the kind of challenging experience the patient herself welcomed—a friend who allowed her boyfriend of a few months to pay for her share of attending an expensive event. The patient went on to speak about the need to be alone in these new situations, that one could not carry out this kind of exploration with another person. Her next set of thoughts was about the uniqueness of analysis, in that she could not do this without me (this was said with an apparent calmness and comfort, reflecting a solid sense of trust in me and in the work). She went on to speak of what I understood to be a sense of optimal distance in the analysis, when she could speak of things without fear that she would be suffocated or that her identity would be appropriated.

"My parents tried to impose their ideas on me—now I fear that more than anything," she explained. I commented that it was almost as if this was about who owned her. The patient responded by returning to the subject of her friend: "If her boyfriend pays for this, then it's as if he owns the memory." I wondered aloud: "Who is going to own your experience and your memory?" And the patient replied: "If I do the work, then I've earned it. Freebies are okay once in a while, but you can't spend your whole life getting them because then nothing's ever your own." I then explored with her whether she might be connecting the feeling of ownership to the sense of feeling genuine. The session continued productively, with the patient reflecting about ways in which she struggled to become certain of her opinions (i.e., that she had something true and good in her mind) before sharing them with colleagues.[7]

This patient suffered from a lack of self-confidence that had seemed to be almost immune to the reality testing provided by her very considerable accomplishments and the positive responses of others to her work. As she herself often noted, it was only the bad stuff that seemed to stick in her mind. One could hypothesize a constitutional deficit either in the ability to have and to hold—which I think unlikely, based on the patient's ability to internalize our interaction; more likely, the patient had lacked the experience of being in an environment that either gave her positive images to internalize or permitted and encouraged her to feel her own. This captured what she and I reconstructed of her childhood. Both parents, it seems, suffered from narcissistic pathology that permitted them to develop neither accurate nor positive mental representations of the patient. The patient described (as one might imagine) significant deficits in their own self-esteem.

Mitrani (1998) addressed this crucial issue. Although she did not speak directly of what the mother is able to give to the baby, she argued that it is necessary for the mother to possess enough self-love to be able to contain the baby's feelings of adoration for her:

> I would suggest that the containing capacity, initially felt to be located in this type of external object—when introjected—leads to the development of an internal object capable of sustaining and bearing feelings of ecstasy and love, an object that might form the basis of the patient's own self-esteem. This aim certainly calls for an analyst who truly thinks well enough of his or her own goodness that he/she is not dependent upon the goodness and cooperativeness of the patient in order for such a positive self-perception to be confirmed and in order for the analyst to continue to function analytically (119).

I have been speaking, of course, of what the infant's original environment provides. What sustains these patterns for the child, and later for the adult, is a more complicated matter as internalized interactions and intrapsychic conflict become more and more active.

Having a Patient

As Abend (1979) described, patients enter analysis with specific cure fantasies. Perhaps the selection of a particular analyst is a confirmation that the patient believes the loop has been closed, so to speak; unconsciously, this analyst is seen as one who can fulfill the conditions of that fantasy. Analysts, too, have fantasies about what they do to or with their patients, although these fantasies have been much less discussed. I have previously speculated, for instance, about the universality of a Pygmalion, or creation, fantasy in both analysts and patients (see chapter 1).

As Akhtar (1995) has cautioned, taking a patient into analysis must be very carefully considered because it is like choosing a person who will become one's permanent neighbor. He suggests that one way to evaluate suitability for analysis (specifically, ego strengths and level of reliability) is to ask this question: Would the analyst be comfortable having this particular person not necessarily as a friend, but as a neighbor, someone who can respect the fence and with whom one can resolve conflicts and conduct other neighborly transactions requiring trust and goodwill?[8] This question captures ego-level considerations, but the intimacy with one's patients goes far beyond this. Smith (2000) writes cogently about the extent to which the analyst does and should become deeply involved with the patient; projection is inevitably involved in the analyst's "necessary and potentially problematic immersion in the patient's world" (110):

> Analysts are not only trying on the patient's world—that is, identifying, like trying on a suit of clothes—but also, in part unconsciously, trying their own world, their fantasies, their clothes, if you like, on the patient.... The analyst checks back and forth, examining the patient's material, gathering evidence, matching it with hypotheses, as he tries to draw as accurate a picture of the patient as possible. That picture is not simply an elaboration of the analyst's fantasy, although analysts vary in their conscious or unconscious capacity of willingness to make this distinction. That said, I suspect that what one finds in the patient is always a mix of oneself and the patient (110).

For me, it is as though each patient comes to inhabit a distinct area of my mind, as though each has his or her own file that can be clicked open or closed; however, while these are files that may eventually be placed in the recycle bin, they can never be permanently deleted from the hard drive. Each file, it seems to me, consists of the collection of memories and associations that I have laid down in connection with that patient. They include both articulated and unarticulated responses. And just as the patient comes to have the parent or the analyst through the internalization of units of experiences of object-affect-self, so, too, does the analyst's having of the patient include all these elements.

To the extent that my discrete experiences of a particular patient might tend to be similar to each other, then I would think of my mental representation as having the quality of a "character." When a given unit of experience with one patient strongly resembles an experience with another patient, I come to a moment when I find myself momentarily uncertain as to what exactly has happened with which patient. It is as though my finger has slipped on the keyboard, and I have unintentionally activated the "find" function; my unconscious has thus clicked open a second file, and

I need to do a bit of reality testing. I ask myself, "*Which* patient said that?" and "*Which* metaphor do I use with *which* patient?" to get myself back into the correct program.

Poland (1998) has noted that he has a sense of trepidation at the beginning of each analysis because he knows that there will be a need to go with the new patient somewhere that the analyst does not want to go. It might seem here that Poland is denying that the element of surprise exists in analytic work, but I do not understand his statement in this way. I believe he may be referring to the certainty of being surprised and the expectation that these surprises will not all be pleasant ones. Whatever our fantasies of cure may be, in order to help a patient, we must be prepared to open our minds and take in whatever the patient wants and needs to put there. We must expect that we will encounter the unexpected. Smith (1993, 1995) writes about the effort analysts make in order to make room for the unexpected:

> However much we may try to approach every hour with some sense that it is the first or only hour, the first hour of the day with a familiar patient is very different from the first hour with a new patient. Like returning to a novel we have been reading, but not today, there is a feeling of coming back to something familiar, familiar transferences, that have an established fact and place in the analyst's life at the moment (1993, 429).

My view is that the appropriate analytic listening stance requires both a sense of the patient as known and familiar and a constant striving to be open to the unexpected.

For me, the process of coming to feel that I "have" a patient in my head happens for the most part unconsciously, although often with much conscious effort. In a lengthy evaluation process, there comes a point when I find that I have stopped taking notes, when I have somehow shifted from interviewer/questioner/evaluator to more of a therapeutic "being with" the patient (although I do not mean to imply here that either stance is ever totally absent from the analyst's mind). I can perhaps best describe this as a sense of "something clicking into place"—that I have found some kind of basic framework for understanding this new acquaintance. For me, it means that the type of work I need to do in the clinical process has shifted. It means that I feel I have reconnoitered enough to slow down and enjoy each view with some confidence that I have the tools to begin to place it appropriately in the total context of the patient's life. Having the patient in my head means that the working relationship is revved up and the engine is running smoothly; I can then attend with greater clarity to episodes when the engine catches or stalls. Poland (1998) similarly describes a feeling of "laying claim to the patient," referring to "the shift when someone moves in my mind from a new patient to *my* patient."

Sometimes, even with much effort, the feeling of having is slow to come or comes not at all. In the several situations in which this has occurred to me, I believe that there was some way in which the patient did not want me to have him or her, did not want to allow the intimacy that would permit a feeling of being understood. These are the clinical hours when I struggle to find the right thing to say, when I feel my intuition and empathy are off. I am not including in this category encounters that took place in my early years as a clinician, in which I simply assumed that I did not know enough to do a good job. Now, I regard this occurrence as potentially an early negative therapeutic reaction, or as representing an enactment or actualization of something in the patient's early life. It is also possible that a particular patient may stir up a countertransference reaction that leads me to foreclose the patient from my mind and, correspondingly, to withhold myself from his or her mind.

Perhaps what I am saying is no more complicated than that the experience of accurate empathy for the patient reflects the achievement of an accurate mental representation—of "having," to put it differently. One patient expressed surprised pleasure when I mentioned a fact about his childhood that he had not brought up in a very long time. He said the fact that I had remembered this information and knew it was important and relevant at that moment meant that I understood him. This patient, who described his parents as never knowing what his worries or concerns might be, was encountering the fact that I "had" him in my mind. The timing of interpretations is certainly relevant, for it is clear that this mental representation must not be a fixed idea, but must change in such a way that we make accurate (for the most part) judgments about what the patient can hear at a particular moment.

I have found that, for this reason, I much prefer converting psychotherapy patients to psychoanalysis over starting an analysis immediately following an evaluation. I suppose that it is, for me, a question of comfort—that I am less anxious about whether I can be a good analyst, and whether the match is a good one, when I feel that I already know the patient well. I suspect it is an easier shift for the patient as well, for the patient already has me in his or her head when analysis starts. With some patients who have a history of emotional deprivation or abuse and consequent difficulties with trust and with object constancy, it is doubtful that they will be able to tolerate the deprivation of visual cues usually entailed in analysis.

I suspect that this process of coming to have the patient in one's head requires the patient's consent. I can think of one psychotherapy patient with whom the process did not take place. A woman in her late twenties presented with a history of emotional and physical abuse on the part of her mother toward herself and all the siblings in her rather large family. To give but one example, she had observed the mother attack the father physically on several occasions. Try as I might, the sense of clicking with her did not occur. Week after week, I seemed to have all the information I needed to form a picture in my mind, but found I had to struggle to be ready for each session. This is in sharp contrast to the way I feel with most of my patients. It is normally almost effortless to feel ready for each session (although I may need to check my notes to jog my memory about the specifics of the last session, if there was nothing in it that struck me as unusual or dramatic). This particular patient left treatment after a few months, acknowledging cognitively rather than affectively the newly discovered significance of her history; she was strongly resistant to taking the stance of empathy toward herself that I felt for her and probably communicated to her.

When I speak about being ready to work with a patient, I am referring to a mostly preconscious knowledge of what the relationship demands of me. After all, we are accustomed to playing different roles in different relationships, the interaction drawing on some and tending to minimize other aspects of one's personality. Having a patient in my mind seems to mean that it is relatively easy to slip into this particular persona. And an important part of my having the patient is knowing how the patient has me. How is this patient able to use me or not? What does this patient require of me? What kind of holding environment does this patient rely on me to provide?

Later in treatment, having the patient also involves the analyst's sense of the patient's potential beyond what the patient can imagine. Just as parents use words with a baby who cannot possibly understand language yet, the analyst envisions the patient's growth before the patient can do so. This is what Lacan (1936) described as the mirror stage—that the mirror reflects an image more whole and unified than the baby feels. However, I am not using this idea in a pejorative way, or (as Lacan did) to emphasize the loss inherent in taking on this image. It is a necessary step in development. The vignette presented earlier demonstrates this phenomenon, in that my liking and respect for the patient extended beyond what she felt for herself. As Loewald (1960) puts it: "The child begins to experience himself as a centred unit by being centred upon" (20).

The Analyst's Position During the Analysis

Although the analytic relationship is most often understood to be a parallel of early developmental phenomena, it is perhaps apt to compare it as well to the situation of marriage. While it is certainly true that marriages gratify archaic as well as adult strivings, there is a fundamental difference—as I noted earlier, we choose our spouses or mates, while we are unable to choose our parents. There is something undeniably sexual and romantic—and uncomfortable—about comparing the analytic relationship to a marriage, yet there is no denying that the level of intimacy and the sense of familiarity with the Other attained in a well-functioning analytic dyad is in many ways similar to that of a good marriage. For the patient, analysis is always in a certain way the most intimate relationship he or she has ever had, in the sense that the barriers to psychological intimacy are generated primarily by the patient and not by social expectations. (This presumes a good-enough analyst who is alert for the way in which his or her unconscious resistances will enter the analytic arena.) And even for patients and analysts in good, well-functioning analytic marriages, the analysis very likely generates more sustained, active talking and listening than tends to occur regularly in the hustle and bustle of ordinary married life.

Psychoanalysis is also like a marriage in its promise of fidelity—that is, there is a guarantee of confidentiality on the part of the analyst and an effort to curtail acting out and to bring things to the analysis first on the part of the patient, thus enacting a kind of forsaking of all others. The trust in a solid marriage derives in part from this security of having the spouse (and of course I do not mean this in the sense of literal ownership and the archaic vow to obey). So, too, does trust in the analytic relationship derive from the patient's confidence in the analyst's promise of confidentiality and devotion to the patient's needs and, for the analyst, from his or her reliance on the patient's commitment to working things through in the analysis.

The patient's primary vehicle for achieving intimacy is self-disclosure; the analyst, on the other hand, shares intimacies in the form of verbal self-disclosure only on those rare occasions when it would seem to benefit the patient.[9] The analyst's contribution to that intimacy rests in his or her actively available and present intellectual and emotional self. In order to do the highest quality analytic work, the analyst must use every fiber of his or her being in the process of listening and formulating interventions. The functioning of an analyst is selfless in the sense of not being selfish—the analyst's task is to focus on the patient's needs—but it requires the intense use of the analyst's self. Despite this requirement of devotion, which is clearly similar to the way good parents attend to their baby, the mature contract—the treatment alliance—is in some ways more akin to the partnership of a marriage than to the actual dependence of a baby on its parents.

There is a paradox here, for as much as we may wish for patients to take from us, to use us, we are in fact helpless to make this happen. To reiterate, "[T]herapeutic experience in analysis is found by the patient—it is not provided" (Casement 1990, 343). All we are able to do is to take an educated and intuitive guess at what conditions may be optimal for any particular patient to find and use the analyst as that patient is able. While we certainly have the capacity to commit soul murder, we do not have a similar ability to generate souls; however, we can provide the conditions under which the patient's motivation and constitution may allow this to occur.

Finally, although it may seem as though it is the analyst who takes care of the patient (and in a sense, this is literally true, both legally and in terms of the analyst's responsibility of safeguarding the analytic process), in reality, psychoanalysis is a partnership between analyst and patient. Just as interpretation is a joint product, a result of the intermixing of thoughts, so, too, are the responsibilities of the patient and the analyst separate but equal, as in a marriage. Childrearing, earning a paycheck, cooking dinner, taking out the garbage, and doing laundry are all essential tasks; an analysis cannot take place without interpretation and free association, holding and being held, maintenance of the frame and enactments that threaten the frame.

The Patient's Experience of the Analyst

As Burland (1996) noted, all children have the right to feel that they own their parents' minds. Similarly, the fantasy of possessing/having the analyst may be vital to the analytic process. This can be reflected in the way the patient uses the actual analytic office space. In a sense, the possession that comes with a marriage is more actual than the possession that accompanies being a child. In the partnership of a marriage, there is a mutual agreement that what is mine is yours. And, as parents know, one has to submit to the reality that what one had thought was one's house is now regarded by one's child as his or her house (and accurately, too, particularly in the teenage years!). It is up to the parent and the analyst not to question the child's/patient's sense of shared ownership—that is, unless and until the house rules have been violated. Some patients, for instance, feel entitled to enter my office even before I invite them in. Some patients get up in the middle of sessions to use the bathroom without an acknowledgment of the coming and going. Adult patients need to feel as though they have free access to and ownership of the analyst's mind, in the same way a child patient may have his or her own drawer for artwork in the analyst's office. As one patient of mine phrased it, it was as though she had a "time-share ownership" of me.

Perhaps "having" has something to do with the thorny issue of "character," which, like pornography, we may not be able to define, but we know it when we see it. When I think about having, I think about the issue of surprise. For instance, as an analysand (albeit one with a certain amount of external knowledge about my own analyst), I could certainly not say that I knew my analyst in the way I know my friends or family. I did not know his particular history, life circumstances, and so forth. And yet, though unfamiliar with the specifics of his background, I came to know almost unerringly his style and rhythm of thought. When the mental representation so well matches the external reality, the sense of having the other person is buttressed. When we are rarely surprised by what another person says or does, this would seem to be a measure of the extent to which we know that person's character.[10]

Things are, of course, more complicated in the clinical situation, for the analyst's relative anonymity facilitates the creation and maintenance of transference illusion—that is, of the analysand's ability to create the analyst that he or she needs. During the analysis, this illusion may be best left unexplored for a time, along the lines of Winnicott's (1951) recommendation not to examine too closely the source of the transitional object. It is also quite possible that neither analyst nor analysand will be aware of the existence of the illusion.

To give an example: In my own personal analysis, I would often make references in my associations to characters and plots from my favorite movies. I was aware, in reality, that my analyst was much more educated about film than I. However, I was not aware until well into the termination period of the degree of illusion in this. My analyst was (to coin a phrase) the strong, silent type, and one way that I read his silences was as meaning that he was instantly familiar with all the characters I mentioned. Undoubtedly, my further associations would jog his memory, even if he had not immediately placed the name. But—and this was my contribution to the maintenance of the illusion—I would never stop to ask if he was following my thoughts, knowing that if he could not do so, he would inquire. I did not ask, that is, until a few months before termination. In fact, he responded that he did not recognize the name of a character I mentioned. My sense of shock was profound, for it made me realize the extent of my illusion. In a sense, the illusion was not all that great, for my analyst shortly did recognize the name, as I had expected he would; but the fact that it had not happened instantly told me that the person I had in my head did not precisely match the external reality. While I thought I had had in mind what was actually there; in reality, I merely had what I imagined to be there. It does seem ironic that, once again, the best way to understand what "having" feels like is to describe what it is like when one becomes aware that this having has been threatened, that it did not obtain in the way one thought.

Being close as I was at that time to the termination of my analysis, it was appropriate that both my analyst and I permitted this optimal disillusionment to take place. Neither my sense of him nor my sense of self was threatened by this mini-loss. And this leads me back to the other side of the coin—the elusive question of what having an Other *does* feel like. Parens (1970) has perhaps come closest to describing what I mean in his paper on inner sustainment. He defines this as resulting from "the dynamic and economic state within the psychic organization that leads to feeling loved and supported from within. This quality of inner sustainment, or its lack, is derived predominantly from early experiences" (223). Inner sustainment, he proposes, "at all ages depends on the character of internal representations, the actions of the assimilative processes, and ultimately the character these impart to ego and superego functioning as well as to self-concepts and identity-formation" (225). Inner sustainment can thus emerge from the experience of having an object in a satisfactory, positively valenced way.

In a sense, I am suggesting that the feeling of Other-having is a building block of such larger and more complicated feelings as inner sustainment. Feelings like security, the confident expectation of being loved, the sense that the Other whom one loves is interested in oneself, and perhaps the very knowledge of being positively cathected and valued by another are also components of having. The notion of being valued might imply that in order to come to feel that one "has" the Other, one must already feel oneself to have been "had" by the Other. After all, "value" does involve a sense of possession.

Termination: To Have and Have Not

In psychoanalysis, of course, the event that throws into relief the issue of having is termination. Much of the literature on termination points to what is, in the context of this chapter, a not-so-puzzling phenomenon—that is, the ease with which the transference neurosis is reawakened. Perhaps this chapter addresses Freud's question about whether analysis is terminable in its proposal that having is more or less a permanent thing. Like bicycle riding, once we learn/have something, it is there forever, unless there are new opportunities to learn and thus alter the mental representation. The permanence of having explains why clinical research interviews of former analysands result in almost immediate resumption of the transference (Pfeffer 1961). Luborsky's research (Luborsky and Crits-Christoph 1990) on transference also contributes to an understanding of this phenomenon—that not only is the mental representation of the analyst permanent, but earlier parental and Other representations in the mind are also evoked. Luborsky and Crits-Christoph note: "Apparently, one's wishes, needs, and intentions in relationships are relatively intractable, yet the expectations about others' gratifying or blocking one's wishes and one's emotional responses to the others' actions or expectations have more flexibility or malleability" (142).

Luborsky also reports that transference content tends to increase rather than decrease toward the endings of analyses that are judged to be relatively successful, as compared with analyses judged to be less successful (Luborsky and Crits-Christoph 1990, 4). A graduate of a psychoanalytic institute who had but little contact with her former training analyst reported that her transference and predilection to have fantasies about him remained quite strong; however, she noted a significant diluting of this tendency after she had actual chance contact with him. In other words, her sense of having her analyst remained more alive in her mind in the absence of data that would reinforce their altered relationship. Social constructivism aside, each new relationship does in some way offer the opportunity for projection and repetition. As Freud (1905) put it: "The finding of an object is in fact the refinding of it" (222).

An analysand approached her first August in analysis with much trepidation; upon exploration, it emerged that she assumed her analyst would simply forget about her during the vacation. The analyst commented that she seemed to feel it was possible for the image of her to be erased from the analyst's mind much more easily than was in fact the case. Patients who have not had healthy experiences of having will doubt that the analyst (and other Others) can or will share such an experience. In these cases, one of the key goals of the analysis is for the patient to believe and to come to rely on the actuality of the analyst's ability and desire to have and to hold him or her. I know that while I may not spontaneously recall all the details of a particular patient's life, there is a way in which I will never forget the essence of any patient I have treated in depth. When we work with patients, we truly make them part of ourselves in some permanent way. We may change them—both they and we hope this will happen—but, without a doubt, they change us. The very fact of mental representation, that the relationship persists in the mind and memory regardless of whether actual contact continues, means that in psychoanalysis, psychotherapy, and all relationships of intimacy and depth, we are always taking the vow: "Till death do us part."

Notes

1. Caper (1997) has written about the development of the sense of a separate self as dependent on the mother's ability to have an Other of her own—that is, the child needs the mother to have a relationship with the father that excludes the child. If this does not occur, then the child's ability to form a sense of differentiation between self and Other is impaired. Caper's argument is essentially an exploration in object-relations terms of Lacan's concept of the name of the father and the crucial role this plays in allowing the child to enter the register of the symbolic.

2. I thank Parens (2003) for suggesting this last point to me.

3. The child will first refer to him-/herself as "me" or as his/her name. The use of "mine" comes next developmentally. "I" is a later achievement (Sharpless 1985, 874; Parens 2003). I would understand this progression as moving from a sense of self as object, then to the concept of possession, and finally to the sense of self as subject. Bergman (1999) does not directly address the developmental sequence of language acquisition in which I am interested here, but his views on the general subject of possession are nonetheless of interest.

4. When I use the term "accurate" here (and later in reference to clinical work), I do not mean it in a positivistic sense. What I have in mind is more the idea of good-enough empathy; that is, the Other's mental representation of the child or analysand will be close enough to the self-representation of the child or analysand that the interaction (the experience of object, affect, and self) will be usable and internalizable as positive. I also do not mean to suggest here or elsewhere in this chapter that all interactions are either entirely good or bad, but rather to state that there is a continuum, with virtually all interactions having ambivalent qualities.

5. As Etezady (1990) wrote in his report of Anthony's presentation: "Even with the most depressed, disturbed or abusive mother, there may have been moments during which the mother was able to identify with the needs of the child, meet them and thereby provide a nucleus of organizing internalization. These small islands of peaceful interaction in a world of turbulence have greater impact on these infants than we have heretofore been aware of" (5).

6. For an example of this, see the section later in this chapter on "The Patient's Experience of the Analyst."

7. As my clinical work described in this vignette suggests, it can be quite helpful to point out to patients for their consideration the ways in which they seem to have or not have the analyst.

8. "Good fences make good neighbors" (Frost, 1914).

9. I do not mean to suggest here that the analyst can know about this with certainty. The process is more one of utilizing the accurate enough mental representation of the patient to make an educated or intuitive guess about what the patient will find most usable at a particular moment in the treatment.

10. I am not speaking here about surprise as written about by Smith (1995). I would term what he discusses "microsurprises"—incidents of unexpected statements, feelings, or insights that occur throughout an analysis. These are part of the ongoing process of analyzing; they do not fundamentally alter one's sense of the identity or aesthetic of the Other, or throw into question the terms of the analytic engagement. By contrast, an analysis could also entail "macrosurprises"—for example, discovering that a patient had committed a criminal act.

Nothing but the Truth

5

Self-disclosure, Self-revelation, and the Persona of the Analyst

THE QUESTION OF THE ANALYST'S SELF-DISCLOSURE and self-revelation inhabits every moment in every psychoanalytic treatment—even though we might wish to believe otherwise. Just as it is not clear exactly what we mean when we use the word self in our metapsychology, I suggest that the referent of "self" in "self-disclosure" is also not without complexities. This chapter will explore the relationship between the information disclosed or revealed by the analyst about herself and the self of the analyst. I am proposing that all self-disclosures are not equivalent and that differentiating among them allows us to define a construct that I am terming the "analytic persona." I believe we analysts rely on an unarticulated concept of an analytic persona that guides us, for instance, as we decide what constitutes appropriate boundaries. To what extent does disclosed information actually reveal something that represents what could be understood as the analyst's identity? What is it that is disclosed? What is the relationship between the analyst's identity as analyst and identity as a person? "Self" is often used in our field as if there were a unitary self we either reveal or not, and as if it were an all-or-nothing issue, when it is more helpful to consider the self not only as layered but also as multifaceted and shifting with each context—to consider, in other words, aspects of self. I propose that bringing the notion of persona to bear on this issue may clarify some seeming contradictions in our understanding of technical and theoretical issues.

Just as the concept of persona denotes a part of a self that represents the whole self in that moment, so too is the title of this chapter complete as is, even as "nothing but the truth" brings to mind its partner phrase, "the whole truth." Our professional ethics call for us to tell nothing but the truth and simultaneously for us not to tell the whole truth. The frame and structure of the analytic setting free us to do just that. The frequency of sessions places an optimal pressure on both analyst and patient to become emotionally intimate; the limits placed on the contact by time, technique, and ethics contribute to the development of that paradoxical "as if" mode of reality that is the hallmark of the transference neurosis. Just as we rely on our patients to be able to walk out the door and conduct their lives in a way that is detached from the regressive experience of the treatment, so too do our patients rely on us to do the mirror image of this. Many analysts already have an unarticulated working concept of an analytic persona, the self we step into as the patient enters the office and step out of at the close of each session. Our attitudes toward self-disclosure and self-revelation can usefully be considered reflections of how we conceptualize an analytic persona. Levenson (1996) succinctly clarifies the distinction between disclosure and revelation:

> To reveal is to allow to be known what has heretofore been hidden (a passive act). To expose is to make public something reprehensible, a crime (we are not dealing with that), and to disclose is to act, to make known an occurrence that has been under consideration but, for valid reasons, has been kept under wraps. I would like to elaborate that distinction. Self-revelation (unveiling) would refer to those aspects of the therapist that are inadvertently or deliberately permitted to be apprehended by the patient. Self-disclosure would be whatever the therapist deliberately decides to show (or tell) the patient (238).

My views are consistent with the distinction Meissner (2002) draws between disclosures that emphasize the real relationship and those that serve to strengthen or maintain the therapeutic alliance. I do not mean to suggest that active, intentional self-disclosure ought to be a regular and common occurrence. Self-revelation, on the other hand, is an inescapable part of every moment. What I am arguing is that certain kinds of disclosures and revelations have reference to part of the analyst's self that belongs to an analytic persona.

Persona: A Definition for Psychoanalytic Purposes

"Persona" as it relates to the analyst's self-disclosures and self-revelations can be thought of in a somewhat pejorative sense. For instance, as Hanly (1998) comments:

> When I look back over the path that these reflections on the self-disclosure of the analyst have taken, I discern a direction toward an attitude of skeptical openness toward self-disclosure. I am not skeptical about the efficacy of timely, sound interpretations. I am skeptical about self-disclosures. They can be damaging to the analytic relationship and the analytic process. But interpreting involves a dimension of self-disclosure that we disregard at our peril and that constantly tests us. This dimension of self-disclosure, which contributes importantly to the therapeutic alliance, constitutes the opacity—the capacity for selflessness—that places the patient and his or her needs at the center of the analyst's interest and occupation. To confuse neutrality with anonymity is to deny the inevitability, as well as the psychological necessity, of being oneself as distinct from being only an artificially contrived, anonymous, professional persona (564).

However, "persona" can also be used in a non-pejorative manner that can clarify our thinking about self-disclosure in the analytic setting. I will use the term to delineate the analyst's available and presented self in a given moment or setting. The *New Oxford Dictionary of English* defines persona as "the aspect of someone's character that is presented to or perceived by others: her public persona." The analytic persona is the self as perceived, or available to be perceived, by the patient. Frank (1997) outlines a prescription for an analytic/therapeutic persona:

> Analytic authenticity demands a willingness to reveal one's personal involvement—not just as an anonymous or understanding persona—but as one who is engaged in, while examining, the fullness of the possibilities that might develop within and between the participants during the analytic interaction. It must be understood, however, that it is never advisable for the analyst to rush eagerly or compulsively to reveal his or her experience to the patient—each impulse, fantasy, accomplishment, or quirk, for example—in order to respond authentically (309).

Let me offer two brief clinical examples that demonstrate the ways in which analysts already use the principles of an analytic persona and "nothing but the truth." Judith Chused (2001) gave a presentation in which she described lovely work with a latency-aged child. The young patient was unable to express certain thoughts and feelings, and Chused articulated them for her as a self-disclosure as if she, the analyst, had been experiencing them herself. During the discussion period, Chused was asked about the extent to which she felt able to use this technique with patients. Her reply was that she could not lie to patients and that she could take on, assume, and articulate only feelings with which she herself could identify.

In other words, if the patient were experiencing something that Chused felt was alien to her, she could empathize with the patient but could not assume the affect state, as she had with this patient. If an analyst is able to conceptualize, form associations to, create metaphors for, or fantasize about something, then this, by definition, represents an aspect of self. In terms of Meissner's distinction between the real relationship and the therapeutic alliance, Chused has presented a particular version of the self-as-object that will enhance the therapeutic alliance. Empathizing clearly must involve identification; I understand Chused's distinction as referring to the strength or depth of her identification.

What I want to stress in this example is that Chused speaks of taking on a role, of playing a part, for the benefit of her patient. She describes a limit to the extent she can do this, and this limit involves what she feels potentially to be true of herself. This is precisely what I mean by the persona of the analyst, that it is a part or potential part of the analyst that is disclosed or revealed to the patient; it does not have to represent the entire truth of the analyst's being, though it must represent something that the analyst is able to assume, if only in fantasy, as part of her self. It is nothing but the truth but not the whole truth. Metapsychologically, we could conceptualize an analytic persona as representing a benign split in the psyche, often a consciously chosen one. Naturally, a persona may be adopted for defensive purposes as well and may reflect an enactment of countertransference (in the narrow sense of an unconscious, and possibly countertherapeutic, response to the patient).

My second example of the use of an analytic persona is provided by Diane Martinez (Brice 2000, 553), who reported on a case in which she had made spontaneous interpretations to a patient. One was that the patient yearned for compliments, but that "the positive effect is gone in thirty minutes—like that old saying about Chinese food." The second concerned the patient's tendency to engage in multiple anonymous sexual encounters while really wanting a more serious relationship. Martinez commented: "Looking for a life partner in the park is like shopping at K-Mart for an Armani suit!" She felt that what she had said had been "foreign" to her, as she in fact thinks differently about Chinese food and knows that one can find designer clothes in unlikely places. Because Martinez herself brings up the question of having stated as true something she was not certain she believed, we need not question whether this ought to be considered a metaphor; if she had considered her statement to be only metaphoric, she would not have been troubled by the way she had presented these interventions.

Martinez is described as uttering both of these statements spontaneously and in a way that was emotionally genuine and meaning-laden to both her and the patient. We could call this acting, perhaps, or we could say that it represents an analyst using parts of the self that are only in part reflective of what she would profess to believe and that have a semblance of truth only in that moment. I would suggest that this acted, created self-presentation is an example of the appropriate use of an analytic/therapeutic persona. Perhaps the aspect of self that is being disclosed here is the analyst's wish to be of help to the patient and her willingness to feel or believe things she ordinarily does not for the sake of that potentially therapeutic moment. So it is as if what is being revealed is something like this: "I say these plausible things that I may believe only in this moment, and they represent what I feel in a consistent way, which is that I want to help you." The choice to make these statements, to include them in the analyst's persona, comes from the analyst's work ego. And to return to Chused's point, there are limits to what she can represent herself as feeling or being.

To look at the issue from another perspective, let us consider the analyst's silences. A patient notices on my car's side window a small Amherst College decal. She talks in session about what it means to her that I had attended such a fine school and chose to spend my time seeing her for a somewhat reduced fee. I do not comment on her factual assumption. Such events are the bread and butter of analysis, grist for the mill in the work of exploring the transference. My silence, I think, is similar to Martinez's remarks about Chinese food and designer clothing. Silence here is an action taken for therapeutic reasons, an action that allows the patient to assume something about the analyst that may or may not be true. Unquestionably, an act of omission (not confirming or correcting a patient's assumption) is not identical with making a statement to a patient that does not reflect one's usual or consistent beliefs. But the two types of intervention involve the building of an analytic persona. What is truthful in my permitting the patient to believe what may be an untruth is my wish to allow the transference to deepen so that the patient and I may learn more about her mind. This may be akin to the social phenomenon of the "white lie." A white lie may facilitate a social encounter, and allowing a patient to believe what may be untrue about the analyst may facilitate the analysis. "Lying," both socially and analytically, however, may express not only altruism but also cowardice, hostility, or masochism.[1]

There are many situations that highlight the extent to which our usual assessment of what is truthful is flexible and situation-dependent. Consider the use of case illustrations in our professional literature. Do you assume that I have just told you the truth in the vignette of the patient and the decal? You probably understand that I may have changed particular facts in order to protect the patient's identity (see, on this point, Ogden 2005). So do I lie when I tell you about this "patient," or do you assume that I tell you nothing but the truth—or a "truth equivalent"—even though not the whole truth? This is analogous, I think, to the notion of saying to a patient something that is momentarily or potentially true in a given clinical moment and context. What does it mean to you that I have not let you know what the truth of the matter is?

I am not suggesting that intentional lying in the sense of saying something to a patient that we know, or believe at that moment, to be untrue is a good thing. What I am arguing is that both in analysis and in everyday life, our feeling of telling the truth is context-dependent and only partially reliable. It is better to accept that what we utter may be only a partial truth even as we believe it to be nothing but the truth or even a whole and permanent truth; the truth of an utterance may reside in the spirit rather than in the letter of our utterance. As Mitchell Wilson put it to me in a personal communication: "Because the analyst has an unconscious just like the patient, it's entirely possible we don't know why we said or did a certain thing. In that sense, we are unreliable in our self-reporting and this possibility must or 'should' be a part of our working attitude. We are always lying 'a little,' it seems to me, even if we mean to speak the entire truth."

Painting our Own Portraits and the Evoked Persona

Inasmuch as I have proposed that an analysis can be conceived of as a creative object, perhaps an apt analogy to my concept of persona can be found in literary theory. What I have in mind here is the way in which, although we know that the author is the creator of the speaker (or narrator) in a work of literature, there is not an identity between the two. In other words, we are not justified in assuming that we may learn more about the speaker than exists within the data of the work itself by studying the life of the author (Beardsley 1958, 238–39). Now obviously this applies to an aesthetic or critical study of the work, as opposed to a psychoanalytic or biographical examination of the author. But it is an important distinction. I am proposing that the persona of the analyst represents a carefully or not-so-carefully studied selection of the self of the analyst, but that what is presented and perceived does not accurately represent the self of the analyst with permanent or global validity. And just as the creator of a work of art does not possess the authority to determine the meaning of the work, what "is" in it, so too must the analyst share that authority with the patient.

Psychoanalysts have long known that patients perceive us in a manner determined by their own character and neuroses. What has been focused on much less is the way in which the analyst, according to his or her own character and neuroses, appropriately structures and manipulates the data about him- or herself to which the patient has access. Even an analyst who tells no specific personal fact (putting aside the fact of the disclosures we make through our office decorations, cancellation policies, etc.) reveals a great deal through the empathy embedded in each and every intervention. The very facts of what we choose to say and not to say and of what we select in the patient's material are of the greatest significance.

Persona, as I am using the term, refers to the sum of all the presentations of self by the analyst that are available to the patient—this includes disclosures and revelations that are intended or unintended, conscious or unconscious, tacit or explicit, and episodic or continuous acts and utterances. Ideally, these presentations will manifest the benevolent manipulation that is part of the new developmental experience we hope to provide (Loewald 1960). Our ethics require that this be done with the best interests of the patient in mind. We can also understand this as similar to the ways in which parents ordinarily speak to their children, giving them information that is age-appropriate, and protecting them from what might be overwhelming—but, ideally, never lying to or misleading them.

Persona, self-disclosure, and self-revelation are characterized by dimensions of deliberateness, temporality, activity, prominence (background versus foreground), and purpose (anticipated therapeutic effect). My office decorations, for instance, constitute an old revelation; if I were to answer a patient's question about whether I have seen a particular movie, that would be a new disclosure. The first is nonverbal, the second would be verbal. The decorations are more or less constant and, while once an active choice on my part, now feel to me to be a more passive and implicit rather than chosen or intentional disclosure. The revelations implicit in my office decor are usually in the background rather than the foreground. And when is a disclosure considered to have taken place? When we "make" it or when the patient perceives it? Of course, as a patient changes she may be able to perceive data to which she had previously been oblivious. And how do we understand "disclosures" within the transference—information we give that had particular meaning to a particular patient, data that are understood within the idiomatic frame of reference of the individual?

We may need to respond as if the patient's perceptions were indeed actual disclosures—this is what it means to allow oneself to be used in the transference. The patient's perception of the analyst's intention is significant too. In other words, does the patient believe that he or she receives "knowledge" of any particular piece of information with or without the analyst's wish that it be known or the analyst's knowledge that it is has been "discovered"?

I believe that even when we think we know who we are in a given moment, or that we can predict our own responses in some future moment, we are likely to be at least partly mistaken. While I do not wish to throw the issue of character entirely out the window, it would nonetheless be problematic to consider the self a knowable, enduring, and stable entity. Simply using the term self so freely does not mean we ought to fall into the trap of believing that we truly understand what such a thing as a self is and whether it exists as anything more than a convenient or necessary narrative construct that saves us from experiencing life as unending chaos. Thus, in what I am saying there is no implication that the persona of the analyst is a pathological construction. It is a reflection of how we all function all the time. As Frank (1997) notes: "Clearly, it is simplistic to think of analytic authenticity merely as revealing one's true reactions to the patient" (307). To a very great extent we always are who we are in relation to the environment in which we find ourselves.

As some disturbing studies have demonstrated (e.g., Milgram 1974; Haley, Banks, and Zimbardo 1973), personality and behavior are to a surprising degree evoked by social expectations. The psychoanalytic setting is not immune to this effect, which can be benign as well as malignant. Let us take, for instance, the use of humor. While it would certainly be best left to others to characterize my sense of humor, it is probably fair to say that I have a tendency to be playful. With some patients I allow this tendency to come through, refraining only from jokes or humor that would be seductive, in bad taste, unprofessional, or otherwise inappropriate. With other patients I would rarely feel tempted to remark on the ironic or humorous side of something—and with some patients such observations would never even occur to me. To use humor is, without doubt, a form of self-revelation, as well as potentially a disclosure, interpretation, enactment, actualization, confrontation, or any combination thereof. Whether I am playful or not in any absolute sense, there is no question that I am "being myself" and revealing myself to each of my patients. But the self I disclose is not a constant, an unvarying monolith. Inevitably, I—and all clinicians— display different selves, aspects of self, or slices of self to each patient and in all of our relationships.

We know that analysts limit the data to which patients have access, and this limiting is taught as the ideal position of the classical analyst. As Freud (1912) put it: "The doctor should be opaque to his patients and, like a mirror, should show them nothing but what is shown to him" (118). We think much less about the way the analyst actively molds the image he or she presents to the patient. As Greenberg (1995) has put it: "Consider the standard injunction, 'Don't just do something, sit there!' That is often good advice, but the implication is that it is possible to do nothing, which seems unlikely to me. . . . The decision, then, is not whether to reveal something or not; rather it is whether I choose to reveal something deliberately" (201).

To take another example, in everyday life I probably act with a normal amount of patience. I am short-tempered or irritable at times with my family, less so with my friends, and very rarely so with colleagues, students, or patients. Some of this comes from the fact that it is easier to suppress, sublimate, or analyze and utilize one's irritation for the benefit of the other person for a forty-five-minute session than it is when one lives with someone. But much of it comes from how I see my role with these different groups—what I want to get from the encounters and what I want to give. I define the encounters differently, I expect different things from them, and thus my threshold for irritation is different. Therefore I am less prone to experience irritation with friends, students, or patients. This means that both the self I experience and the persona I present in different settings are rather different. As Schafer (1983) notes:

> In our best work as analysts, we are not quite the same as we are in our ordinary social lives or personal relations. In fact we are often much better people in our work in the sense that we show a greater range of empathizing in an accepting, affirmative, and goal-directed fashion. This observation suggests that there is a kind of second self which we develop, something comparable to the narrative author. Robert Fliess (1942) has called this second self or at least certain aspects of it the analyst's work ego. This second self is not and cannot be discontinuous with one's ordinary personality; yet, it is a special form of it, a form that integrates one's own personality into the constraints required to develop an analytic situation (291).

Levy (2005) has addressed the question of naturalness in the analyst, pointing out the inherent unnaturalness of the analytic attitude. He suggests that the increasing comfort that analysts say comes with experience may reflect not so much a natural ability as a greater technical expertise. I would suggest that the analyst's adjustment to the analytic stance reflects the development of an adaptive analytic persona that includes an acceptance of the technical demands of our craft. Because so many of our technical and strategic decisions occur unconsciously or preconsciously, they may feel to us as though they are natural; they also appear to have qualities of artistic judgment. This does not mean, however, that these components of an analytic persona do not in fact result from practice and experimentation with tactics and techniques, as well as with certain inherent elements of the analyst's character. As Glick (2003) puts it: "[W]e both discover and *create* in ourselves a natural psychoanalytic style" (379; emphasis added).

Levy and Inderbitzen (1992) state that "both abstinence and anonymity are relative, there being inevitable gratifications and revelations about the analyst that are part of the intimate, long-term relationship between analyst and patient" (992). Renik (1995), too, emphasizes that disclosures on the part of the analyst are inevitable and that what matters is "how to manage the unavoidable condition of constant disclosure" (468). And as Aron (1992) puts it:

> Anonymity is never an option for an analyst. You can sit, but never hide, behind the couch! . . . What is critical is not whether the analyst chooses to reveal something at a particular moment to a patient, but, rather, the analyst's skill at utilizing this in the service of the analytic process. Is the analyst or, more accurately put, is the particular analyst-patient dyad able to make use of the analyst's self-revelation in the service of clarifying and explicating the nature of their interaction? (480, 483)

However we designate it, as persona or as a second self, the analyst presents some version or mix of self-qualities to patients, and it is important for patients to have a sense of having and being permitted access to the analyst.[2] We give of ourselves in each interpretation, and we give the patient something to grab onto. If patients did not feel us to be present in an active way, most of them would leave treatment.

Clinical Illustration: A Range of Disclosures of Areas of Self and Shifts in the Analytic Persona

The following vignettes describe a range of disclosures and shifts in the analytic persona. I would like to emphasize that I do not assume that the patient perceived my interventions and disclosures exactly as I intended them to be perceived. No interaction within an analysis can be entirely "real" and free of multiply determined meanings for both patient and analyst (see Boesky 1990).

In one session, a graduate student who had come to analysis because of a writing block described a chapter of his dissertation that he was working on. He spoke with great detail and clear inspiration, and at the end of the session I commented on what appeared obvious to both of us, that the patient had essentially composed the chapter in the session. The following week, under pressure to complete the chapter, he demanded to have my notes from the session, reasoning correctly that I take practically verbatim notes. He said that he felt they belonged to him. This felt entirely different from a patient requesting to see the clinical record—to which the patient does have legal rights, whether or not it would be beneficial for him or her to exercise them. I encouraged the patient to explore his feelings, and I wondered aloud what might be getting in the way of his recalling what he had said. This did not lead to a diminishing of the intensity of his request or to an increase in his curiosity about why he would make such a demand. This was most unusual for this patient, who was generally eager to explore the workings of his mind. After a couple of sessions, the patient chose to sit up rather than lie down, saying that this issue did not feel to him as though it was something to be analyzed. I identified with the patient in his frustration, having had my own share of difficulty with writing; yet I also felt a mounting sense that to comply with his request would damage our relationship and put me in the position essentially of a stenographer. It felt to me like an impasse—and a test having to do with my conviction in the therapeutic process. My clarifications and interpretations were not helpful, and the patient became more and more focused on the imagined solution that my notes would provide.

It was unusual, to say the least, for this patient to seem so inaccessible, and I was uncertain how best to proceed. I decided that as I did not know what was really going on (this occurred about a year into treatment), the only thing I could do was to regard my reactions as vital data that were emerging from the interaction between us. Other clinicians may well have reacted quite differently, both in how they might have experienced such a request from a patient and in how they decided to respond to it. I decided to speak to this patient about my own very complicated reactions. I confirmed that, as he had thought, I did take down much of what he had said (as opposed to writing a commentary) and that I would sometimes also jot down my own associations or reactions. I also said that my writing was a routine part of my way of working with a patient who was on the couch.

As such, it felt as though he was asking me to share something private, as though someone had demanded of him that he hand in his research notes in lieu of his fully articulated and written thoughts. In other words, he was asking for access to my private process rather than to my end product. He considered all this carefully and, much calmer, said that he liked the way I worked and did not want to do anything that would make me have to change it. He added that he would not want me to feel constrained about what I wrote because of the chance that he would later ask to see it; he quickly recognized that this was not to his advantage. It seemed to me as though the patient had retreated from what had felt like an attack on my analytic persona—an attack fueled by his own needs, anxiety, and disappointment (not to mention his wish to take my writing for his own). The patient returned to the couch, and we were gradually able to focus on what was happening in his mind to obstruct access to his previous creative mental state, as well as on what confronting me in such a way might have meant.[3] The point of this vignette is that I spoke with candor about my method of working and my feelings. The disclosure felt to me to be deep, intimate, and yet somehow not of a personal nature.

My purpose in taking this action was to restore three things: first, the conditions under which I could best help this patient; second, a threatened therapeutic alliance; and third, the patient's belief that my refusal to accede to his demand was in his interest. Perhaps the major rationale for disclosing in this very deep way was to explain to the patient a stance I had taken that I had no other way of explaining and that he had the right to understand. The circumstances required me to deepen the way in which I made myself available to this patient, although I did not feel that the disclosures involved material that was fundamentally outside the analytic endeavor. Let me contrast that with a different type of disclosure, one that involved my personal life outside the analysis, also with this patient.

On one occasion this patient remained in town over a long weekend in order not to miss a session. He had been undecided about his plans for a long time and we had spent many sessions exploring what this signified; a central issue involved his fear of intimacy and his willingness to make a deeper commitment to the analysis. After all this, I ended up needing to cancel this session due to an ill child. I knew I would not be able to reach the patient in person at that particular time, so I left him a voicemail message to the effect that a pressing family situation had come up unexpectedly, that I would have to cancel, and that I was sorry to have to do this at the last minute. It is extremely rare for me to cancel appointments, I struggled about doing so in this situation, and I felt terrible about it.[4] Before the next session, I reflected on how best to handle the situation in the upcoming hour. This was different from in the impasse about the notes; here I felt that I had initiated an action that could reasonably be experienced by the patient as hostile, in that I had violated the safety and reliability of the therapeutic frame. When we next met, I waited to see how the patient would respond. As I had expected, he spoke of his rather strong responses to this event—I had not told him in my message the specific reason for cancellation beyond what I described above. This patient had taken an important step in deciding to attend a session, and I then acted in a way that said, in essence, that the session was less important to me than it was to him. In the session, I felt that it would be appropriate for me to explain a bit beyond this and said to the patient that I would be willing to do so. After he indicated that he had also felt this way, I offered him the choice of whether he would like me to do so first or to talk about his feelings and fantasies first. (My rationale for giving the patient this option, I think, had to do with returning to him the measure of [or illusion of] control of the time that my cancellation had violated.) He chose the latter option and guessed that it probably was a child's illness. After he had reached what seemed like the end of his associations to this, I confirmed that his conjecture had been correct.

The point I wish to make is that this disclosure—necessary and appropriate, I think—felt entirely different from the disclosure described earlier about the way I work and my need for privacy. This second was a disclosure of an element of my personal existence rather than of my existence with this patient. But both of these disclosures felt extremely intimate. The purpose of this second disclosure was to prevent a malignant and actual power imbalance from developing that would impede the understanding of how these issues had already been alive for the patient. It felt as though it would be disrespectful of me not to confirm his conjecture. Here, as in the first illustration, the effectiveness of the disclosure had to do with the restoration of the therapeutic alliance, which cannot exist if the patient feels that he has been treated without common human decency; my real-relationship disruption of the work required real-relationship decency in response. My disclosure had given the patient access to information I would not normally have allowed to enter my analytic persona; however, my cancellation had already amounted to a disclosure-equivalent, and one that had had a destructive effect.[5] I had introduced a turbulent element and it was incumbent on me to return the analysis to its previous state in which the patient was the primary source of turbulence.

Another type of disclosure seemed to be from an intermediate area. At the beginning of my work with this patient, he had not asked me much at all about my credentials. This became an issue later on, as we came, over many months, to understand how powerless he felt in knowing almost nothing about me and what it would mean to him to have some information. He said he needed to know about my academic and professional training, as well as some other things, such as whether I was married or single. In some ways I felt as though it made no difference at all whether he had this information or not, as I knew we would explore the meaning for him of whatever I said or did not say. But what would have mattered a great deal was the sense of coercion I felt, and the way in which revealing this information would have constituted a submission to a demand. I did not give him any information about my family, but did tell him about my educational background and professional training. And I found myself including my undergraduate school and major. It was clear to me as soon as I spoke that this information belonged to an area outside my analytic persona. That I included this is most curious. I understand it as an expression of my wish to be transparent and known—and also perhaps as representing an unconscious submission. What I did not yet know was whether my choice here also represented my side of an ultimately productive and beneficial enactment. In other words, was it for the patient's benefit? While I would not consider this to be a boundary violation, it did feel like a boundary crossing. But, at that point in the treatment, perhaps the patient needed to know that I was doing something out of the ordinary. Indeed, he did immediately speak about this information as being extremely revealing and in a different category.[6]

A disclosure of the first kind—active, conscious, and intentional in real time, and disclosed for the benefit of the patient—about my note-taking and need for privacy, is a disclosure of aspects of myself that in some sense already belong to the patient. It is a revelation to the patient of something that in fact is already in the room with him, whether he knows it or not and whether I have articulated it or not. I would say that this is a disclosure of the persona of the analyst. The persona is the area of the analyst that he or she is potentially willing to let the patient have, and this willingness to be had is for the benefit of the patient, for predominantly altruistic reasons. I want to distinguish this from the notion of self-disclosing a reaction that one believes is the result of a projective identification. In this situation, the analyst is revealing something that is thought to have originated from the patient. There is, of course, no definitive way to tell the difference (although there may be a sense of foreignness to some projective identifications). In fact, the projective process can only work by what the patient stimulates in the analyst that is already there to be acted upon. It is the fact of the analyst's willingness to be acted upon that I wish to emphasize.

The second and third vignettes describe disclosures of material not normally in the therapeutic arena, information that neither the patient nor I would normally introduce in this fashion. Both disclosures emanated from outside what Hoffman (1994) has referred to as the "relatively protected position" of the analyst that is "likely to promote the most tolerant, understanding, and generous aspects of his or her personality" (199). When I intentionally move beyond this more customary position, I have the sense of needing to act with special caution, of being on alert, of being in new territory. It is this feeling that alerts me that I have moved outside my analytic persona.

The openness of self that I feel within my analytic persona is a part of my regular stance with patients. It stands in stark contrast with the feeling that I ought not reveal something that comes from outside the analytic arena. It feels different to speak openly with patients about my responses in session than it is to reveal even a seemingly trivial piece of personal information. I believe that the question is not how deep a particular disclosure is but rather whether it comes in a segment of self that I had planned to include in the therapeutic encounter. We have drawn a line; we have selected what will go into the persona we present to patients. When we cross that line, we (and our patients) feel and know it.

Ethics and Disclosures

We withhold information for the patient's immediate benefit and in order to maintain for ourselves the conditions under which we feel we can be most helpful. When we do not respect these requirements, this results in boundary crossings and potential boundary violations.[7] While some disclosures would clearly constitute boundary violations and others would be minimally personal, there is a wide middle ground in which analysts determine their own lines. For instance, if a patient begins to talk about a movie he has just seen and asks me if I have seen it, I may well choose to answer—it will depend on what I think the patient needs of me and what I judge will contribute most to (or might impede) the flow of material at that moment. However, if a patient considering an abortion were to ask about my personal experiences or opinion, I would not consider answering. In the first instance, I have revealed what I have done on a recent evening and perhaps my taste in film. In the second, I would be revealing a fact that might imply to the patient that I did or did not approve of her morality, what I have or have not done in my private life, and so forth. These issues certainly have relevance to who I am but in their specifics are not properly a part of a conversation with a patient. They represent private and intimate facts, information I exclude from what I am willing to share. Jacobs (1999) distinguishes disclosures about his whereabouts on vacation, or the books he reads, from his disclosures of fantasies he has during a session that seem related to the patient's material. I believe that the distinction he draws is virtually identical to mine between what falls outside and inside the analytic/therapeutic persona.

We make determinations all the time about which parts of ourselves we make available to the patient and which we withhold. What about a therapist who tells his patient that he is about to be married, that he has been divorced twice, that he has twins (whose pictures are in his office), and that he is about to put central air conditioning in his vacation home? In a sense this information is less intimate than my telling a patient about my feelings within a session—that is to say, less close to sharing one's self. Yet I would consider the other therapist's disclosures to be violations of professional boundaries and his definition of a therapeutic persona to be highly problematic. For another example, a colleague of a relative sought treatment with me. I had to consider whether I would be willing to work with someone who had met members of my family and knew already so much of the actual circumstances of my life. I felt something akin to nakedness as I contemplated this possible treatment, and this reveals the degree to which I feel I need a certain privacy in order to be dressed and professional with a patient. I chose not to enter a situation in which I would not have the power to withhold information that I felt it would not be to the patient's benefit to know and that would undermine my ability to work. It would have left me inadequate room both for the patient's fantasies and for me to create an optimal analytic persona.

Persona Disclosed, Self Anonymous: The Emotional Availability of the Analyst

The relationship of the analytic persona to the self may be akin in certain respects to that between narrative and historical truths. One need not be certain of the relationship between persona and self and narration and history for psychoanalysis to be helpful. In the final analysis, what matters is that emotionally effective interactions have taken place between analyst and patient. The effectiveness of those interactions rests on there being an emotional genuineness rather than a truthfulness that would be identical to or as broad as what would exist in any other relationship the analyst might have. The analyst's emotional authenticity counterbalances offering few factual disclosures. And emotional authenticity requires us to tell nothing but the truth but certainly not the whole truth, even if we were able to know it ourselves.

Let me try to articulate this paradox by looking to my experience of my training analysis. Of course no training analyst can ever be completely anonymous to a candidate analysand, because both share membership in the same institute. This said, though, my analyst was quite classical in technique most of the time, elegantly reserved and unrevealing of personal information. I knew some facts about him before treatment began but learned very little during the analysis itself. Yet, despite this, I came to feel a sense of security that I knew him very profoundly, that I could predict his reactions, and that I knew everything about him that truly mattered. After a time, I was rarely surprised by anything he said or did within the analysis, that is to say, anything that emanated from his analytic persona.[8] My patients say similar things to me, how strange it is that they feel they know me well even without knowing the sort of things they are accustomed to knowing about other people with whom they are close. Patients come to know such things as kindness, empathy, humor, curiosity, demandingness, wit, relentlessness, the tendency to show off, and self-awareness. And in the light of familiarity with these qualities, knowledge of specific facts, revelations, or reactions in specific sessions may contribute rather little. I felt that I knew my analyst well despite the fact that he remained largely anonymous to me. Perhaps it is accurate to say that I knew him only profoundly—or that I knew only his analytic persona.

A clinically effective analytic persona may include much self-disclosure or very little and vastly different mixes of self-disclosure and self-revelation. Let us consider a proponent of self-disclosure such as Owen Renik (1993). Renik at times includes in the cards he plays face up (Renik 1999) his opinions about the patient's issues or actions.

> All in all, I find that self-disclosure for purposes of self-explanation facilitates the analysis of transference by establishing an atmosphere of authentic candor. When my patients experience me as saying what I really think—about them, myself, us—they respond in kind. All too often, it seems to me, clinical analysis deteriorates into a game in which the patient feels free to bring up all sorts of ideas, without taking any of them quite seriously. When the analyst does not disclose what he or she is really thinking, and

> disclose it as completely, as straightforwardly as possible, the patient is not encouraged to do so either. Disavowal gets built into the analytic discourse from both sides, and the patient's exploration of his or her experience is vitiated by a speculative, hypothetical, "as-if" quality. My experience is that the hardest thing for a patient to do is to discuss with his or her analyst profound convictions about the analyst's real character, to tell the analyst the sort of things that the patient suspects the analyst probably hears from friends and family members (Renik 1995, 493).

However, the "Renik" who is disclosed to the patient is not identical to Renik; the persona Renik that is available to the patient bears the same relation to Renik, the person, as the narrator of a novel bears to the author. What Renik "really" thinks is determined by the situation and his role—in other words, it reflects his analytic/therapeutic persona. And, in focusing so intently on how much Renik may disclose, we may forget how much he does not disclose or reveal.

If we then turn to a very different analyst, Axel Hoffer (1985), we see a different mix. Hoffer believes that the analyst's role should be limited to conflict elucidation, leaving the patient the freedom to decide how to resolve problems. He believes that the analyst should exclude his opinions entirely, although he does not see absolute anonymity as necessary to this kind of neutrality. I must include here a personal view of Hoffer, because I believe it is essential to understanding his ideas. I believe that Hoffer's manner (and thus his analytic persona) conveys a thoughtfulness and respectfulness that would color even his "neutral" interventions. So although Hoffer may disclose few opinions and little information, this may be much less frustrating to patients than his colleagues would guess. The composition of one variety of analytic persona may provide an empathic availability that may in certain respects be equivalent to that of a very different sort of persona. As Frank (1997) notes: "[T]he useful limits of the analyst's authenticity are strongly influenced by the analyst's personal comfort level, and some analysts can uncover far more about themselves than others in a productive fashion" (310).

The patient's perception of the analyst's emotional availability and benevolent intentions toward him or her plays a crucial role and can affect the degree of comfort the patient has with the analytic persona as defined and limited by the analyst. The patient I have described in the series of vignettes above believed, for various reasons, that I was intentionally and cruelly withholding myself from him. He felt that there was a master/slave dynamic in our relationship, that this was the reality as opposed to his interpretation of the situation, and, most important, that I had structured things in this way and desired them to be so. In a sense he was correct insofar as he wanted me to make available factual information that I deemed had little to do with my emotional availability.[9]

It is the affective feel of a disclosure that lets me know whether it comes from within my analytic persona. When a patient asks me a question that involves access to my private person, I feel a bit jolted, taken aback, surprised. For example, a patient asked me as he was leaving a session if I was Jewish; another patient asked me if I was a skier. No doubt part of the jolt comes from the need to think quickly, to understand the significance of the question, and to weigh the meaning for this specific patient at this moment of answering or not answering. But I believe that part of my sense of surprise comes from something else, and that relates to this question of how open I keep myself to my patients and the extent to which I feel that my thoughts—my self—belong to the patient when I am with him. It also has to do with how open I am at any given moment to aspects of myself that I had not thought to be immediately relevant to the situation. To confront a personal question that demands information from my existence away from the patient requires that I shift from one dimension of self to another. And it is this mental demand, I think, that results in the sense of being taken aback that I experience. It requires me to shift from a dimension where I am allowing my thoughts to run unimpeded, in which I am totally open to the patient (whether or not I choose to share all my thoughts), to a dimension of self that is not currently active in my mind. It is as though the patient has called on me to open another file on the computer, one I was not working in. And so I then face the question of whether to expand the persona that I offer the patient and of how to explore the persona that the patient may have in fantasy. Whether I decide to make a disclosure depends on my best judgment of what will promote the therapeutic process and what is needed to maintain, protect, or build the therapeutic alliance. It has to do with what constitutes neutrality, a boundary crossing, or an empathic rupture for this particular patient at that specific moment. As Frank (1997) writes: "In a strict two-person sense, it is not analytic anonymity that makes possible a new relational experience, but the analyst's authenticity tempered by the asymmetry of the analytic relationship. Authenticity here refers to the analyst's genuineness, to the truthfulness with which one responds or represents oneself. It also addresses the question, Is one being true to oneself?" (285)

Persona Grata

We shape and rely on an analytic persona in order to function for our patients. We also use and accept as a certain kind of reality the transference persona that the patient assigns us; and we allow ourselves to be used in this way. No matter how much we reveal or disclose about ourselves, we also retain aspects of the classical neutral-anonymous position; our actual status as experts and the unobjectionable positive transference toward a healer or shaman are necessary components of therapeutic effectiveness. Our persona comprises material both conscious and unconscious, intended and unintended, transference-based and real. We sometimes reveal our persona and sometimes ourselves, the latter at times when we are forced by events or patients to expand our analytic persona.

How we delineate the self we present to patients and the self that we may potentially disclose is a personal as well as a theoretical matter. What defines this as a professional decision is the orienting criterion of respect for the patient's needs. But within the analytic persona—and within the bounds of the techniques, goals, discipline, and art of psychoanalysis—we have the potential to be creative and to use ourselves fully and with great freedom. And we may accept, even welcome, the concept of the persona—a construct many analysts may already use and one that helps us give credence to the ways in which we tell nothing but the truth.

Notes

1. On another occasion, a patient looked my name up at Amazon.com and "discovered" that I had written many books. As it turns out, there is another Susan S. Levine who has written on sex therapy; I had written one book on psychoanalytic theory. I did clarify this to the patient, who had wondered whether I had in fact written all of those books. If the patient had not inquired directly and if this issue had emerged well into treatment, I would probably not have provided the information. In this situation, at the beginning of treatment, it felt as though providing this information to the patient fell within any patient's appropriate need to know the credentials of a potential therapist. However, my needs were also involved—I felt uncomfortable with allowing this patient to make an incorrect assumption about my area of expertise.

2. My chapter "To Have and to Hold: On the Experience of Having an Other" considers the importance of the patient's feeling a sense of ownership of the analyst and feeling, in a corresponding way, that the analyst holds the patient in mind.

3. Rachel Kabasakalian-McKay has noted (personal communication) that this vignette describes a negotiation between analyst and patient. The patient had been considering the "chapter" as solely his creation and reducing me to the role of

stenographer. I was attempting to hold to the ways in which the content of that hour was also a co-creation. The notes had come to symbolize this co-creation: "For the analyst to disclose as she did the investment of her self in the process of that hour ('holding out' against being reduced to the role of a stenographer)—and in the relationship with the patient—seemed to facilitate the patient's recognition of her, specifically of her own subjectivity in relationship to him. This seemed to shift him away from viewing her in the instrumental way that he had for the previous several sessions." I would add that the patient may have identified with my defense of my own work process.

4. The vignettes in this chapter are skewed insofar as they present unusual events in my clinical work, events that pushed me to respond in ways that were also unusual.

5. Almond (1995) has an interesting take on the effect of the analyst's forthrightness:

> Forthrightness, another means of emphasis, might seem in conflict with selflessness and anonymity. It is not. The difference is between "*I* noticed that you seem cheerful today" and "I *noticed* that you seem cheerful today." That is, the focus remains on the patient. Forthrightness counters learned inhibitions on directness in social situations. A major function of socialization is to train us not to make direct, confrontational statements to people about their impulses, or how they defend themselves characteristically. "You are acting aloof and distant to protect yourself from feeling sad" is not a comment that would be welcome at a cocktail party, or on a bus. But in analysis we want directness—the analyst's forthrightness models for the patient, encouraging directness about affects, fantasies, and thoughts about the self and the other (479).

6. The first and third vignettes may make it seem as if the patient's curiosity and my disclosures occurred in quick succession. This was not the case. We continued to explore analytically the significance of the first event for years. The matter of my training had come up numerous times before my disclosure and we continued to work on it long after.

7. An enactment, for instance, may well involve a crossing (as in my revelation of my undergraduate training). This may be an important and productive part of the process. However, if it is not recognized as such by the analyst, it has the potential to be damaging to the patient.

8. I was quite surprised to discover the type of car he drove, which seemed not to fit what I knew to be his style; then, after the analysis, I was also surprised by certain administrative actions he took within our institute.

9. I wonder if this bears on the pressing need at times to make disclosures of various facts to borderline patients (the patient in this vignette was not borderline). The more primitive the emotional and cognitive functioning, the less able the patient will be to accept symbolic rather than concrete availability or "giving."

In the Mind's Eye

Or, You Can't Spell "Psychoanalysis" Without C-H-A-O-S

6

In my earlier chapter, "Beauty Treatment: The Aesthetics of the Psychoanalytic Process," I explored why I love doing psychoanalysis through a comparison of one case in which the analytic process had gone well and another in which it had not (although, contrary to what the unsuccessful surgeon would say—that the operation was a success but the patient died—the patient did, in fact, get better). My conclusions were that psychoanalysis shares many characteristics of artistic objects; the process that occurs between analyst and analysand is the object that can be considered to be potentially aesthetic. This is the object that exists in the analyst's mind's eye, I argued. We can only see our patients' patterns in our mind's eye, symbolically, represented by words and images rather than numbers; we can only represent our images to others similarly, through words and the affects and associations they may evoke if we choose them well.[1] Although in certain respects I acknowledged that psychoanalysis partakes of a scientific method—for instance, in the ways in which the analyst formulates interpretations utilizing theories and then testing them with the patient—I presented psychoanalysis as essentially a hermeneutic discipline. It is thus very peculiar for me, in following an aesthetic sensibility, to be linking psychoanalysis to an unmistakably scientific position—although one that emphasizes a post-Heisenberg, postmodern view of science. There is a productive tension between the art and the science of interpretation in the practice and theory of psychoanalysis—and that this tension also exists in the so-called hard sciences. It is ironic to think of returning psychoanalysis to the realm of physics and mathematics after a long period in which Freud's attempts to link the laws of the mind to those of science have been downplayed.[2] While a discipline of language and mind must ultimately be "scientific" or "mathematical" only by metaphor, the mind must be linked more than metaphorically to the brain, the functions of which rest securely within biology.

Analysts are essentially pattern seekers. We listen to stories and to affects. We look for repeating themes within stories and between stories that have no manifest similarities. We listen to our patients and simultaneously to ourselves, trying to determine when our internal story and the patient's external story are facets of the same story. We listen to stories about the present and look for similarities to stories from the past; we listen to stories of the past and seek to discover similarities to what is occurring in the give-and-take of the analytic dyad. Analysts regularly see themes repeated in each of these domains. And we start to wonder what is going on in an analysis when the patient's associations do not flow freely between these three areas. Traditionally, it is transference interpretation that has been privileged; within psychoanalytic politics, this represents the orthodox position on technique and the theory of therapeutic action. One hears stories of analysts who never make any intervention that does not include a reference to "here" or to "you and me." One implication of this chapter is that as long as the patient is affectively invested in what he or she is talking about, it may not matter so much whether transference is the explicit subject of the interpretation; I am suggesting that all mental phenomena essentially reflect the same mental content and underlying themes. If the transference relationship is both real and a displacement, then so are the extra-transference relationships. Whatever we interpret or clarify, we are addressing a version or a piece of the same pattern. I am also suggesting that the either/or one-person vs. two-person psychology debate can be largely laid to rest in favor of a both/and accord. If we consider patterns as both residing in and being expressed by individuals and as having been influenced by and continuing to influence the patterns of other objects, the resulting perspective gives us freedom to focus on whatever piece makes the most sense therapeutically at any given moment—and to do so without theoretical or clinical inconsistency or confusion. The theory of everything, in psychoanalysis as well as physics, may not be a single theory but rather an overlapping collage of theories.

I will address four iterations of this notion of pattern: first, the unconscious fantasy/model scene/repetition compulsion emanating from the patient; second, the analytic process that takes place between the patient and the analyst and the multiple levels and scales of its manifestations; third, how we represent the first two iterations in our clinical discourse; and fourth, how we do so in our metadiscourse, psychoanalytic theory. Analysts and other clinicians have written some excellent papers about chaos theory.[3] Many aspects of the topics I will discuss have been explored in these previous essays. I am perplexed about why chaos theory and fractals have not caught on in our field, as the connections seem so striking to me. I wonder if the problem may be that chaos theory seems too abstract and too distant from daily clinical experience. My approach is from the macro/aesthetic/visual rather than the micro/mathematical perspective, and I hope to make the intuitive and affective relevance of chaos and fractals crystal clear.

Benoit Mandelbrot named fractals in the 1970s, the Latin *fractus* meaning a broken stone:

> Fractals are geometrical shapes that, contrary to those of Euclid, are not regular at all. First, they are irregular all over. Second, they have the same degree of irregularity on all scales. A fractal object looks the same when examined from far away or nearby—it is self-similar. As you approach it, however, you find that small pieces of the whole, which seemed from a distance to be formless blobs, become well-defined objects whose shape is roughly that of the previously examined whole (Mandelbrot in Hall, ed. [1993], 123–24).

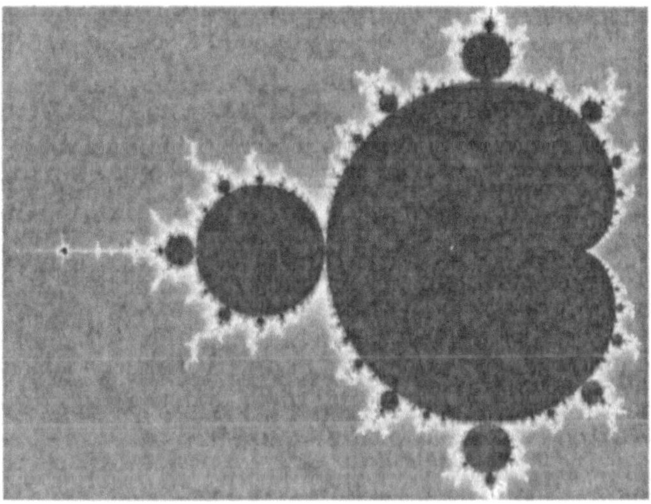

The Mandelbrot set, shown above, is an image of the solution to a particular sort of equation. It has been called "the world's most complex mathematical object" (Briggs, 1992, 26).[4] These types of equations try to answer questions and describe objects that cannot be translated into linear differential equations, a differential equation being the mathematical method of describing change. Fractal images are the representation of the solutions of nonlinear differential equations. Fractals are naturally occurring shapes that can be described by mathematical formulae. Many traces (though not all) of naturally occurring chaotic processes leave fractal patterns. Think back to high school geometry and all those graphs of lines and curves. In these mathematical problems, a change in one of the terms of the equation results in a predictable change in the solution. This sort of geometry does not do a very good job of representing real world phenomena whose boundaries change at an irregular and unpredictable rate. Think of ocean waves and shorelines, the structure of living organisms and organs such as cauliflower, ferns, lungs, population growth patterns, and fluid dynamics.

Fractal, chaotic phenomena are best understood visually, even for mathematicians, physicists, and engineers; this permits an overall pattern to be discerned that overrides the superficial confusion and lack of clarity about the significance of individual events or points. I had found fractals fascinating for years, but had first seen a fractal animation only recently.[5] I happened to watch a movie on a DVD, *The Bank*, and I found the menu image riveting. It was an animation of a Mandelbrot set. The animation focuses on the large bulbous section of the set, zooming in so that one sees finer and finer detail; one recognizes in a tantalizing just-beyond-one's-grasp way that one is seeing something repeat itself. One sees tiny bulbous shapes embedded within the paisley, spikes, and curlicues. Then just when one thinks one is about to "get" the pattern, to be able to say, "Oh, I now see what the organizing principle is," the focus shifts from the fine detail, back out to the large bulbous shape, and the understanding one had felt about to achieve seems to be once again beyond reach. The sequence repeats. I could not get these sequences of images, with the accompanying curiosity, excitement, satisfaction, and frustration, out of my mind, and I came to realize that they captured for me the affective feel of doing psychoanalytic work. I began reading about fractals and discovered that they were mathematical representations of solutions to nonlinear differential equations.[6]

Just as there are many forms in nature that assume fractal or fractal-like structures, similarly these are the naturally occurring "forms" taken by the human mind and human relationships. The functioning of the mind is also complex, rough, and nonlinear. Language and meaning-carrying action (that is, action that can ultimately be described in language, or approximately described) are the manifestations of our dynamic, nonlinear processes. As one writer put it: "Fractal geometry describes the tracks and marks left by the passage of dynamical activity" (Briggs, 22). He was using "dynamical" to refer to the natural world, of course, but is the mind—the psycho-dynamic—not also rooted in the natural world? I am asserting that the application of fractals and chaos theory to psychoanalysis is appropriate both on metaphoric and scientific levels.[7] For this first assertion about metaphoric value, little proof but usefulness or interest of the explanation is needed; for the second about scientific value, it seems to be unlikely that any form of human functioning would entirely escape the laws that appear to govern the natural world. Even though the mind's functions may appear to transcend the natural world's laws of structure and measurability, it is inescapable that the mind is brain-based. Naturally occurring phenomena may possess fractal-like self-similarity and scaling rather than strict mathematically defined fractal dimensions. It is in this category that I wish to situate the functions of the mind, of the psychoanalytic process and of the psychoanalytic discourse. The tension between the aesthetic and scientific views is captured by the anonymous ditty: "What is mind?/It doesn't matter./What is matter?/Never mind" (Zeman 2002).

When I refer to a postmodern science, I include as one of its major contributors the relatively new discipline of chaos theory. Chaos theory is the name given to the constructs that result from the examination of non-smooth and irregular—nonlinear—phenomena. But "chaos" turns out to be something of a misnomer, for there turns out to be an underlying order, which, while not predictable, is not without specifiable structure. It was through studying weather patterns and attempting to make precise forecasts that the science of chaos theory was born. Edward Lorenz discovered that even though it was impossible to make accurate predictions beyond a few days, there was an order within the disorder. This order-within-disorder is normal for our world and is what allows us to know with a fair degree of certainty that Miami will not have a white Christmas this year; however, it would be normal for the weather to be in the 80s or in the 50s.

It turns out that for humans, too, a bit of irregularity—chaos—is more normal than absolute regularity. Sometimes excessive regularity represents a pathological state, as in an epileptic seizure, whereas a slight degree of randomness is more normal and healthy. For instance, an EEG image of a patient going from normal state to seizure would show three separate segments in readings taken from sixteen places on the scalp. The beginning segment would represent a normal, awake/alert/eyes-closed state, characterized by tracings that are within a certain range but display no strong or regular pattern. In the second segment, a seizure begins, and the tracings would show a distinct pattern with high spikes that represent groups of neurons beginning to fire synchronously. It would be increasingly regular and non-chaotic as the firing neurons essentially recruit fellow neurons into the rhythmic firing. This is highly pathological. The patient blinks and is out of touch with the environment. The final third segment would show a state of exhaustion in which the brain cells have exhausted themselves metabolically. The tracings would be clearly disorganized.

For an example comparable to the seizure, consider severe obsessive-compulsive disorder or paranoia. The repetitious nature of perceptions and behavior serve to contain anxiety but rob the sufferer of the possibility of responding to the world in fresh and creative ways. One could conceptualize the healthy self or the healthy ego as permitting a balance between how overwhelming the world would be if we perceived every stimulus as unfamiliar and a constricted state in which nothing can be seen with new eyes.

Another discovery of chaos theory is that a small change in one of the inputs in a system may lead to huge differences in the result, a phenomenon known as sensitive dependence on initial conditions. For instance, two sticks dropped simultaneously over a bridge into a flowing brook alighting a few inches apart will be highly unlikely to be the same distance apart twenty feet downstream. For a psychological example of sensitive dependence on initial conditions, consider how different the personalities of siblings or even identical twins can be. Unlike in linear phenomena, the result from a single input does not result in a predictable output. For another example, imagine the force required to open a jar with a stuck lid. I continue adding force as I attempt to open it. Nothing happens. And then I apply a tiny increment of additional force, the lid suddenly moves, my elbows move outward, and I drop the jar. Think, too, about the onset of an eating disorder in a teenager that appears to be triggered by a single remark. A visiting relative might comment on how a fourteen-year-old girl is starting have a womanly shape; less benignly, someone might ask a teen if she's put on a little weight. These types of remarks will not always set off an eating disorder, and it impossible to predict when they will. Yet we do know that it is a strong enough possibility to suggest that it is not wise to comment on the weight of a teenage girl. This is the domain of un/predictability that is called chaos.

Patterns and the Unconscious

Psychoanalysts cannot know exactly what specific details will comprise the next iterations of a patient's conflicts, yet once we have a working formulation we can often predict the patient's patterns. We may be thus both surprised and not really surprised by what happens next. We sometimes know when material has activated a patient so much that he or she is likely to call before the next session. What is harder to predict is when major shifts in organizing fantasies will occur. Imagine interpreting a conflict over and over to a patient each time that certain conflictual patterns appear in his or her anecdotes about various relationships and in the experience in the transference. The patient is under the sway of an organizing unconscious fantasy. The conflict continues, then, one day, something clicks, the patient gets it, and is able to interrupt the painful repetitions. The power of that unconscious fantasy has been ruptured and the patient's mental life in regard to that particular subject is organized by a different set of assumptions.

We will probably have no idea of when our interpretations will take effect, but we believe they will, someday. This belief, itself, contributes to our fractal pattern in the form of our tone and affect. Perhaps even the frequency of psychoanalytic sessions can be understood to reflect our clinical understanding of this sort of emergent, synergistic phenomenon: It takes a great many tiny initial inputs, at short intervals, in order to maximize the possibility of disproportionate change—like the lid of the jar coming off. Four times a week for three years may be more valuable and change-producing than twice a week for six years. For instance, I might imagine a severely traumatized or borderline patient as being stuck in experiencing characterized by splitting into positive and negative valences or other black and white bifurcations. It is as though the patient is stuck in a pattern dominated by two opposing gravitational forces, unable to see the universe of possibilities outside.

Another valuable concept from chaos theory is that of the attractor. This can be understood as an invisible organizing force with gravitational or magnetic effects. Its dimensions reveal themselves in the image of the fractal.

The image[8] below is of a Lorenz attractor, which one can imagine as a portrayal of borderline dynamics—the patient swings back and forth between positively and negatively valenced mind states. Gleick (233–34) uses the metaphor of the pinball machine to explain the notion of the attractor, stressing that the initial positioning of the plunger determines which, of all the possible routes, the pinball will follow. However, the number of available routes is limited by the structure of the machine. I utilize the idea of the attractor as the parallel within chaos theory to the psychoanalytic concepts of unconscious fantasy, the repetition compulsion, or the model scene. The initial creation of possible routes for the perception of new

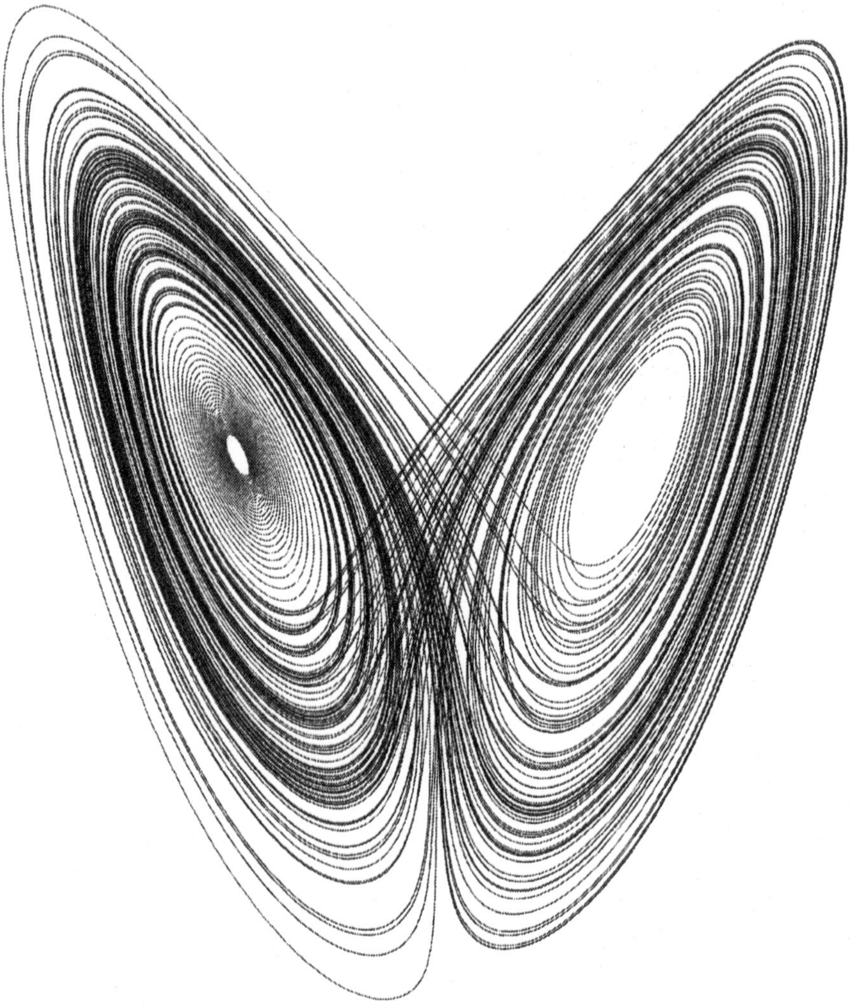

Daniel Schwen, Wikimedia Commons, CC-BY-SA-2.5

experiences takes place early in life when formative emotional patterns of relating and internal somatopsychic response are laid down.[9] These set up the structure of the pinball machine and perhaps the tendencies of the plunger. Psychoanalysis—as well as other intense, traumatic, or repeated new experiences—makes it possible to change the angle of the table (to continue Gleick's metaphor) or perhaps even break through the walls, demolish one of the knobs, or alter the strength and position of the plunger. A patient will only be able to permit an alternative attractor to take hold after a sufficient number of interactions with me and with significant others have occurred—interactions, that is, that rupture the hold of the previous assumptions—the unconscious fantasy—about the self and the world.

A lovely analogy to the problems of psychodynamic complexity and unpredictability can be found in the history of the discovery of complexity in physics and astronomy. In Newtonian physics, the problem of the movements of any number of celestial bodies was, in principle, solvable by calculation of the gravitational forces. However, Henri Poincaré showed that Newton was incorrect and that the so-called three-body problem was not solvable (Murray, in Hall, ed. [1991], 98). It is impossible to predict the movements of three objects, as three celestial bodies act in a random or chaotic manner. Psychoanalysts are familiar with a similar complexity of the interactions of three terrestrial objects, whether we think about this number as associated with the Oedipus complex or pre-Oedipal conceptualizations of the infant and the parents. The multiple interactions and complex influences upon each other make it impossible to predict the vicissitudes of the family constellation in any specific situation.[10]

Scale and the Psychoanalytic Process

I would like to address two characteristics of fractals and their relationship to psychoanalysis, beginning with self-similarity. Fractals display a high degree of self-similarity at all levels of micro- and macroexamination. This means that the structure appears not identical at each level of magnification but that there are identifiably similar shapes and patterns; sometimes the pattern is so large that it can be difficult to discern quickly which segment one is seeing in any specific view. There are three related psychoanalytic concepts that come to mind: the repetition compulsion, transference, and enactment. Enactment refers to the transference-countertransference interaction that results in a joint playing out, rather than interpreting in words, of the analysand's conflicts. Countertransference and enactments are understood now to be inevitable and, if handled appropriately, powerful therapeutic events. As an analyst listens to and participates in a patient's material, a pattern emerges. The analysts interprets or clarifies; the intervention is effective or not; and then the cycle begins again and may even repeat itself in the patient's response to the intervention.

Imagine in your mind's eye a fractal animation as you read the following vignette. A young woman in analysis had been reared by her grandmother, an upbringing characterized by traumatic losses, loneliness, and constant demands to live up to grandmother's expectations. In this session, some years into the treatment, she mentions recurring memories of her grandmother giving her painful enemas. She falls silent, I continue to listen, staying silent myself. She then comments, with an edge to her voice, that she doesn't want to go on talking about this; I ask if she can say more about that feeling. She says she feels a flash of anger and doesn't want to give me what I am asking for. I recognize that there has been an enactment, that my attempt to analyze what is in her mind has become the equivalent of her grandmother giving her the painful enemas when she did not want to give up what was inside of her. Then it was bowel movements, now it is words, thoughts, and feelings. I am aware that I am about to push her, that I want to probe even more deeply, despite her having told me she does not want to go there or do that. I comment that she seems to feel as though I am like her grandmother, trying to get from her something she doesn't want to give. She seems to understand this and begins to talk, with feeling, about how she must have felt as a little girl during the enemas. She then is silent for a moment and her breathing slows; it is a relaxed silence. The pattern that had become large and clear to both of us has disappeared as her associations go to seemingly unrelated matters, and I await the appearance of the pattern's next iteration.

The elements of the equation[11] are several: an incompletely remembered memory, a set of associated affects, and an external situation and object that are close enough emotionally to the template that they can be used to enact the original or model scene (Lachmann and Lichtenberg 1992). And although I cannot discern it in the moment, it is likely that a microanalysis of the patient's words, linguistic structure, and body language would demonstrate an essentially similar form. Virginia Teller, a linguist, and Hartvig Dahl, a clinician and researcher, illustrated this phenomenon in their close study of transcripts and audiotapes of a psychoanalysis (Dahl and Teller 1986). And on the macro level, it would be possible to discern the same pattern if we examined a period in the analysis of a week, a few months, or longer. For example, a patient of mine was so masochistic that he had to undo each insight and each step forward in the outside world; he would typically interrupt his own speech and associations by criticizing his choice of words. It is understood by analysts that a thumbnail sketch of a patient's history will reveal essentially the same characteristic conflicts and dynamics as a detailed history or as an individual session. Analysts often say that everything one needs to know about a patient is there in the initial interview if one looks closely enough. I think it correct to say that even what is remembered is also repeated at many levels of structure and content within speech acts and activities.

Gladwell, in his popular book *Blink* (2005), summarizes much research demonstrating this phenomenon of similarity at all levels of scale in human interactions. For instance, it is possible to make only slightly less accurate predictions from a very brief video recording about the success of a marital relationship or whether a particular surgeon will be sued than it is from watching a more extended encounter. Brief tapes of professors with the sound removed elicit identical assessments of the quality of teaching as longer tapes and as the actual semester-long classes (Gladwell 2005, 12–13). Gladwell's argument is about the power of the unconscious to derive information, but he also demonstrates that there exists information in very short segments that can provide virtually the same information as that available in longer segments. The fractal pattern can be discerned no matter the scale. He writes of how Tomkins was able to look at the images of the faces of members of two tribes and determine correctly that one group was peace-loving and the other characterized by hatred (Gladwell 2005, 199–200). Apparently, the neurology and biology of facial expressions encapsulate in a fractal fashion the sociology and psychology of different cultures.

Individuals develop their template for experiencing themselves and the world—their fractal structure—in the early months and years of life. The essential pattern forms early and is well established by the close of the Oedipal period. We can speculate that a human fractal equation might look something like this; the question marks represent the variability in strength, and the plus and minus signs represent healthy/positive/adaptive and unhealthy/negative/maladaptive valences of each of elements:

> Somatopsychic elements x ? (+ and/or -) + experiential elements x ? (+ and/or -) = individual adult template of self/other experiencing + basic mood/character + existing pattern-reinforcing effects of new experience + pattern-altering effects of traumatic or strikingly unexpected new experiences

Somatopsychic elements would include genetic tendencies, innate psychological/cognitive/intellectual endowment, intrauterine influences, and drives. Experiential elements would include relationship with parents/early caregivers, physical difficulties/illnesses, family stress level, intergenerationally transmitted phenomena, and the influence of the community and broader environment. And, as is the case in the creation of a fractal image, the outcome or template creates the frame of reference through which further data are filtered—the solution of each equation gets plugged into the next equation—and a self-perpetuating and self-similar pattern develops. I would posit that individuals have a threshold level beyond which new experiences hold the possibility of altering existing patterns. This threshold could be reached by traumatic events—that is to say, positive or negative events that, either by intensity or by power of repetition—overwhelm the existing symbolic lexicon, the existing defensive structure, and the ego's ability to cope.

Individuals vary widely in how ingrained their patterns are. If we look back to Dorothy, in my extended description of a single session (in chapter 3), we can see a similar unfolding and interpretation of a pattern with a patient who has the ability to utilize the insights to fuel change. The work with Eliza, on the other hand, offers an illustration of a patient who is stuck on one side of a pattern. I tried mightily, over a long period, to help her shift to another point of view, but I was unable to intervene in such a way as to shift the pattern. One way to picture the mutative process of psychoanalysis is to imagine that its various elements—the emotional impact of the relationship with a new object, the creation of or strengthening of an observing ego, insight into one's wishes, fears, and defenses—act to change the inputs of the equations that describe the fractal pattern. The old equation varies in how stable it was, and so different individuals require different mixes, intensities, and repetitions of interventions. Well-understood and -interpreted enactments may be the most powerfully mutative, because they have the quality of feeling as though they are both within and outside of a transference—that is to say, they both exist in the present and represent the past. The preference that analysts have for transference interpretation may be due to the fact that we can relay more on our perceptions when we are participants in the process. For the patient, however, many extra-transference events have the requisite intensity, clarity, and affective engagement to be interpretable and mutative.

Inputs to the patient's standard working equation and fractal pattern can be changed. Consider the vignette above about the young woman who remembered her childhood enemas. What occurred here? She repeated her standard fractal pattern with me. I felt an uncharacteristic sense of probing or forcing her. I reflected on this and recognized her attempt to repeat her fractal pattern, her template of the world, with me. I put words to it; I describe what her equation was instead of collaborating in its enactment. In other words, I blocked the pattern developing in the way that it had occurred for years. This had two potentially mutative effects; first, the patient's experience was different from what she expected, and second, I helped her put words to the event. The patient had an opportunity to do some reality testing of her template and to find that is was incorrect, and she had the opportunity to expand her observing ego. Both of these effects make it more likely that her fractal pattern is very slightly altered in a way that will reduce her attempt to repeat with the same frequency or intensity and will improve her ability to recognize when her perceptions of the world are colored by her own expectations.

Dimension and Psychoanalytic Aesthetics

The second characteristic of fractals that I would like to relate to psychoanalysis is their dimension. Fractals have what is called in mathematics a Hausdorf dimension of between one and two. The Hausdorf dimension is a means of measuring the dimension of a mathematical object. For instance, the dimension of a point is zero; a line resides in one-dimensional space; a plane in two dimensions; and a cube, of course, in the familiar three-dimensional space in which we live. Let us try to conceptualize an optimal range for the analytic process, or even for the mind itself, in terms of fractals—that is to say, of a particular ratio of order and chaos. Analysts are well aware that there is an optimal range of stability and instability in the analytic process. This is often spoken of in terms of anxiety—the patient must experience enough anxiety to motivate him or her to do the work of analysis. But this also must be balanced by a sense of safety (as I argued in chapter 2). A patient who is cognitively concrete with little capacity to be aware of fantasies would have a dimension closer to a simple line or curve; a patient who was psychotic or in a manic state might appear to be a filled-in plane. In either case, an analytic conversation may not be possible. The parent-child match, too, may be shaped by this preferred dimension or range. We know that a needy and demanding infant will do much better with relaxed and secure parents than with parents who have above-average unfulfilled narcissistic needs of their own. Parents are more capable of forming effective relationships with certain types of infants than with others.

I believe that this dimension or range—in clinical work, in personality, and in parenting—can be thought of as an aesthetic. I am extending here the argument I made in chapter 3 on the aesthetics of psychoanalysis. To illustrate this point, let us turn our attention for a moment to the artistic modality of painting. It has been argued that Jackson Pollock's drip paintings during a sustained period possess fractal characteristics. They are self-similar at different levels of magnification, and these magnifications demonstrate the same Hausdorf dimension of between one and two. In other words, the drip paintings from this period, far from being random, reflect a repeated and identical combination of chaos and order. In Pollock's case, both his creation and our appreciation reflect an unconscious aesthetic.[12] The patterns in Pollock's work share certain features; they are similar to each other and self-similar at different levels of scale in ways that are comparable to naturally occurring fractal-like object; they share a "scaling signature" rather than perfect fractality (Cernuschi, Hersinski, and Martin 2007) As Cernuschi and Hersinski (2007, 84) describe the interaction between Pollack's physical characteristics (height, arm length, etc.), the brushes and other tools he used, the canvas size, and the fluid dynamics of paint. They comment: "The discovery of scaling regularities in Pollock's work provides . . . a powerful indication that his work, both in terms of its technique and ethos, is reflective of the underlying order of the physical world."

Let us take the small leap from paint to words. The act of speech involves an idea or impulse in the preconscious and conscious mind, which is then expressed through language. The language is shaped by the vocabulary and the personality style of the speaker—the tools and the palette. And the listener likewise brings his own apparatus to the encounter. Speech and acts that are meaning-carriers are created by the conscious and unconscious mind, forming patterns that are clear to any listener as well as meanings only available to one listening with the third ear. Lear's concepts of swerve and break are especially well-suited to this image (Lear, 2002). "Swerve" describes the process of the mind's free associations and meaning-making, and "break" the interruptions of those thoughts produced by resistances. Back and forth, smooth and interrupted. These are the intrapsychic mathematical equivalents of the plotting of a fractal pattern, the jagged human geometry.

I believe that each analyst has a similar unconscious aesthetic, a preexisting mental representation of what an analysis should "look" or feel like in terms of its fractal structure, its degree of smoothness and complexity. This may be true, too, of each analytic school or theory. Theory may be understood to be describing the sort of pattern that is likely to develop under certain circumstances. The constituents of this equation[13] would include the complexity of language, the free (that is to say, psychodynamically determined) back and forth flow between present and past, transference and external reality, reporting of "reality" and fantasy, richness of language, gestures, and physical experiences. The analysand must be able to participate in the formation of patterns without excessive, uninterpretable, or otherwise inaccessible resistance to allowing them to develop. It could be said that even the resistance to patterns is a pattern, as I suggested in my earlier chapter in which I wrote about a patient, Eliza, who created an absence of an analytic process. I speculated that she might have been analyzable by another analyst who was better able to appreciate her aesthetic of emptiness. Another way of stating this is that her fractal pattern and ratio of simplicity to complexity was so far outside my preferred range that we were badly matched. I believe there is always a negotiation that occurs within each analytic dyad over what this range will be. Analysts speak of a patient being "in" analysis, and I think this may reflect the dyad having attained a satisfactory solution to the negotiation of the dimensionality of the work. Andre Green speaks (Green 1975, 3) about the patient needing to learn to speak the language of the analyst, but perhaps it is also a matter of learning to be an analysand within the aesthetic of the analyst. For example, one could conceptualize the analyst's anonymity as part of this equation[14] insofar as it relates to the patient's level of anxiety, motivation to continue to free associate, and the facilitating of the formation of transference fantasies. Analysts vary widely with regard to how much self-disclosure they regularly include in the analytic persona, and patients also vary widely in how much self-disclosure they require or can tolerate from the analyst.

The analyst is part of the chaotic pattern rather than a separate, detached, objective observer. The art and science of the analyst is in calibrating one's participation in the pattern-making so as to maximize the possibility that the pattern created reflects more of the analysand's fractal structure than that of the analyst's—and in being aware enough of one's own fractal pattern to be able to tell the difference. True neutrality or non-participation, the tabula rasa, is impossible.[15] It is also undesirable, because if we were able to attain it, it would impede the development of the patient's fractal pattern. A child's fractal pattern, or aesthetic, or character, after all, always develops in counterpoint to and conjunction with the corresponding elements in the primary caregivers. And analysis, finally, must be about helping a patient understand himself in relation to external reality. The effort to help a patient understand and alter his or her preferred fractal dimension or pattern in relation to the reality of the analyst (reality within the transference as well as with the "real" relationship) creates a necessary and desirable tension in psychoanalysis insofar as it replicates the conditions of real life in a non-traumatic fashion.

For a commercial application of this notion of the personal aesthetic, or preferred dimension of experience, consider the phenomenon of Netflix, or a similar service. How does the computer program "know" what films to recommend? As soon as one subscribes to the service, Netflix invites one to rate as many previously viewed films as one has time to do; then one is invited to rate each new film after it is returned. As soon as one does this, a window pops open with recommendations, and all films are accompanied by a certain number of stars—Netflix's guess about whether the subscriber will like each option. While I have no idea how the mathematics of the program work, it must be based on some calculation of what one's taste, or aesthetic, is as compared to those of the millions of other viewers who have rated films similarly.

In the Mind's Eye of the Analyst: Re/presenting Psychoanalysis

The third and fourth iterations I will address have to do with how we describe our clinical work on the clinical and theoretical levels. When we write our cases up or present them to each other, we try to make these unifying themes clear. We try to follow the narrative line of the unconscious; this is one reason that psychoanalytic case reporting is such a difficult task. Even as we attempt to render into words the mind's eye image we have of an analytic patient or relationship, we cannot follow the traditional unities of time, space, and action.[16] The three unities of psychoanalytic case reporting are the transference relationship, the extra-transference "reality," and the past. Words are insufficient to capture all of the sensory and intellectual parts of the experience simultaneously. As I noted earlier, analysts are able to discern patient's dynamics equally well from a brief summary of the situation, an extended history, a detailed report of a single hour, or the description of a single enactment. In a sense this is not at all surprising; no matter how much an analyst thinks he or she might be describing an objective external person or event, the report is in reality of the analyst's experience of that patient. So perhaps it is incorrect to say that an analyst's report can be "of" a patient and his or her patterns. That report must be of that fractal pattern that involves the analyst as well as the patient. We are participant observers, always, and we are not immune to the principle set forth by Heisenberg. We cannot measure movement (analytic process/progress) without including ourselves. Even for us to measure position (an evaluation at any given moment), we must acknowledge the gravitational force of the existence of the interviewer. When we study our case reports, we can see evidence of our involvement in the fractal pattern in such areas as what we choose to include in or omit from the report, the order in which we choose to report various elements, even in (if we take notes during sessions) what we choose to write or to omit. When we discuss cases in supervision, we not infrequently see a parallel process occur, in which we replicate the dynamics of the patient or the dyad with the supervisor.

For example, my supervision on my work with Eliza (a control case) felt awkward and frustrating in a way that I believe was similar to how she felt in analysis with me. The discourse about our cases, whether written, oral, or intrapsychic, reiterates the fractal pattern of the treatment. When we write psychoanalytic case studies, we are attempting to describe a fractal, the residue of a chaotic process. We are attempting to represent a jagged, rough, irregular line pattern as a smooth narrative, while simultaneously retaining the turbulent, non-smooth, chaotic qualities of the treatment.

To move to the last iteration, I propose that the image of the fractal may serve as a unifying construct for the field of psychoanalysis itself—theories that may sound completely different and incompatible are showing images of different sections of the fractal. The superiority of any theory, I believe, has less to do with any absolute correctness than with how a theory seems to fit the fractal structure of the interaction between a specific analyst and patient. We have already imagined as fractals the patterns of the individual mind and patterns of the analytic interaction; would it not follow that larger social interactions would also share chaotic and fractal qualities? The interactions analysts and other clinicians have as we discuss and argue over our theories could be seen as possessing characteristics of fluid dynamics or chaotic traffic patterns. We are all going in the same direction, we follow the same road, but it is difficult for us to see the similarities between our thoughts and behaviors and those with different theoretical approaches. Likewise, the theories we create and espouse emanate from our study of the same subject matter—the human mind as we imagine it to function and as we "see" its manifestations. It is certainly not new to point out the ways in which all psychoanalytic theories to a great extent follow similar patterns—they each must account for the same observable phenomena. For instance, observations of toddlers at the age of approximately eighteen months give rise to conceptualizations such as the anal phase, rapprochement, and the mirror stage. There are different narratives leading to each label, but in my mind's eye, each narrative is simply putting different words to the same fractal formation. Perhaps the mirror stage focuses on the curlicue section of the fractal, rapprochement on the bulbous section, and the anal phase on the contrast between a paisley-like form and a pointed area. But all of these areas can be seen as part of a unified self-similar fractal form, if one steps back and takes the long view. Thus, I do not see that it is inconsistent for an analyst to use a variety of theories in his/her work—and I do not see it necessary to have to account for doing so or to have to make the different theoretical narratives appear to mesh. I believe that chaos theory, and specifically the fractal narrative, can serve as a psychoanalytic theory of everything, scaffolding for our own grand unified field theory. The fractal image includes self-similar, but not identical, theories with overlapping areas of strengths and complementary differences.

One of the longstanding problems for those who wish to consider psychoanalysis a science is that of prediction. Neither clinical nor theoretical knowledge permits the sort of specific, testable prediction that a "hard" science is thought to require. The "hard" sciences are dependent for their apparent hardness and definitiveness on the regularity of the subject being studied. When jaggedness and roughness are studied, then we enter the realm of chaos and nonlinear equations. But there is an assumption that the hard sciences are entirely hard, when in fact, like the Brooklyn Bridge, their piers rest on a soft foundation. It behooves us to reconsider how hard the "hard" sciences actually are. Even a discipline as seemingly objective as mathematics has been conclusively shown to be dependent on intuition as the only source for verification of its most basic axioms. Gödel, nurtured intellectually in Freud's Vienna but not the Freudian Vienna, proved in 1930 that arithmetic's assumptions cannot be proven within the discipline of arithmetic (see Goldstein's summary, 2005, 128–35, 198–99). In this sense, we might consider the analyst's art and craft—and the entire field of personality measurement studies—as being roughly equivalent to arithmetic. Even though such psychological studies as Benjamin's (1974) are impressive in the extent to which they can delineate and measure personality, because the measurement terms are verbal, the conclusions cannot be understood to attain what could be considered objective validity; the terms themselves are subject to the subjectivities of the observer and reporter of their existence—even if the question of defining the terms can be resolved to a high degree of reliability. Our dependence on intuition for our basic axioms may make our field more similar to rather than less valid than the fields of science and mathematics. And, finally, let us accept that, just like physicists, we cannot measure what we study precisely, since the states of mind and processes are moving targets that are altered by our very presence.[17]

Our short-term prognostications can be uncannily accurate—analysts quite often know what their patients are going to say before they say it. And we know that something as apparently small as the few words of an interpretation can have an enormous and long-lasting effect—we just cannot predict which few words will do this. We don't know if the Brazilian butterfly's wings will cause a tornado in Texas or in Toronto, but we know there will be something somewhere (Lorenz 1979). It is in this way that the science and aesthetics of chaos theory apply beautifully to psychoanalysis. And yet our attempts to render in words the affects and images in our mind's eye of a psychoanalytic process are always incomplete. In the words of Levenson: "It is unfortunately true that any clinical presentation, particularly a written one, is so adumbrated as to have the vitality of a pinned butterfly. Any effort to 'present' clinical material is simultaneously an act of courage and a murder. Even unkinder things may be said of attempting an exegesis of someone else's presentation" (1983, 72).

Viewing psychoanalysis as a chaotic and nonlinear as opposed to a Newtonian science may relieve some of the pressure analysts feel to answer to the challenge of "evidence-based" medicine movement—this pressure resulting from a sense of inferiority that our work is based on intuition and interpretation. Are precise predictions of the complex systems of the self, of self and object, and of self and object in the larger environment attainable at all? Let us acknowledge without apologies the intuitive basis of our work. Is it necessary to determine any absolute superiority of one psychoanalytic—or other variety of—theory over others? Once we have weeded out claims made by our theories that are clearly not confirmed by empirical observation (such as Freud's conjectures about female psychology or Klein's hypotheses about infantile cognition), our theories are more alike than not. Let us enjoy the beautiful and self-similar perspectives of our clinical experiences and psychoanalytic theories.

Notes

1. Long after I wrote the initial version of this chapter and devised its title, I cam across the following remark (Stewart in Hall, ed. [1991], 44): "But above all chaos is beautiful. This is no accident. It is visible evidence of the beauty of mathematics, a beauty normally confined to the inner eye of the mathematician but here spills over into the everyday world of the human senses."

2. I am, of course, not the first to attempt to resume this effort. Lacan and Bion also attempted to create mathematical discourses about the psychoanalytic process and the structure of the mind, but they did so before the advent of chaos theory and its ability to describe nonlinear phenomena.

3. These include Galatzer-Levy (1995), Eidelson (1997), Levenson (1994), Moran (1991), Spruiell (1993), Busch (2007), Quinodoz (1997), Sander (1983), and Harris (2005). The last two authors deal primarily with developmental applications.

4. Quotation in Briggs without reference.

5. Googling "fractal animation" (via Google images) will lead you to this site: http://images.google.com/images?q=fractal+animation&hl=en&btnG=Search+

Images. The website www.seraline.com will lead you to a mesmerizing fractal screensaver; I thank Diane Trees-Clay for telling me of this site.

6. Understand that, to mathematicians, the animation of fractals apparently has only aesthetic, as opposed to scientific, significance.

7. See Quinodoz (2007) on the question of theoretical models and metaphors.

8. http://images.google.com/imgres?imgurl=http://upload.wikimedia.org/wikipedia/commo ns/thumb/f/f4/Lorenz_attractor.svg/300px-Lorenz_attractor.svg.png&imgrefurl=http://en.wikiversity.org/wiki/School:Mathematics&h=300&w=300&sz=89&hl=en&start=4&um=1&tbnid=5hRb59IzSmEkoM:&tbnh=116&tbnw=116&prev=/images%3Fq%3DLorenz%2Battractor%2Bopen%2Bsource%26um%3D1%26hl%3Den%26sa%3DG.

9. Busch (2007) uses the fine term, "pathological attractor sites."

10. Einstein, of course, later posited gravity to be analogous to a bending or depression in the surface of a plane; illustrations of this phenomenon appear similar to some illustrations of the attractors as basins.

11. I am using this term in a common-language sense here that is intended to evoke but not be understood as identical to the strict mathematical usage.

12. Taylor (2002) reports that viewers prefer a dimension of 1.3–1.5, regardless of whether the observed pattern is of natural, mathematical, or artistic origin. Jones-Smith and Mathur argued against Taylor's conclusions while Taylor responded with a defense of his methods and conclusions and questioning of the questioner's assumptions (November 2006) then defended by Taylor. The controversy stemmed in part from the issue of whether Taylor's conclusions were solid enough to be used in the determinations of authenticity of paintings thought to be by Pollock (for a summary, see article in the *New York Times*, December 2, 2006). Whether or not Pollock's work (or a segment thereof) can be determined to be fractal, and whether or not a mathematical analysis can be used to authenticate authorship is almost beside the point.

13. See note 11.

14. See note 11.

15. We cannot do as Freud instructed, to be "opaque to the patient and show them nothing but what is shown to [us]" (Freud 1912, "Recommendations to physicians practicing psycho-analysis," SE: 12: 121–44, 118).

16. Freud, in the Dora case, essentially pioneered this sort of narrative. Let me note that I am not suggesting that Freud's treatment of Dora represents how I or any analyst I know would work.

17. Following the Heisenberg principle.

References

Abend, S. (1979). Unconscious fantasy and theories of cure. *Journal of the American Psychoanalytic Association, 27*, 579–96.

Akhtar, S. (1995). Personal communication.

Almond, R. (1995). The analytic role: A mediating influence in the interplay of transference and countertransference. *Journal of the American Psychoanalytic Association, 43*, 469–94.

American heritage dictionary. (2000). http://www.bartleby.com/61.

Anthony, E. J. (1990). Dandelion children. Paper presented at the Association for Child Psychoanalysis and the Vulnerable Child Workshop, Santa Fe, New Mexico, April 6.

Aron, L. (1991). The patient's experience of the analyst's subjectivity. *Psychoanalytic Dialogues, 1*(1), 29–52.

———. (1992). Interpretation as expression of the analyst's subjectivity. *Psychoanalytic Dialogues, 2*, 475–507.

Balint, M. (1957). *The doctor, his patient, and the illness.* New York: International Universities Press.

Barratt, B. B. (1994). Critical notes on the psychoanalyst's theorizing. *Journal of the American Psychoanalytic Association, 42*(3), 697–725.

Beardsley, M. (1958). *Aesthetics: Problems in the philosophy of criticism.* New York: Harcourt, Brace & World.

Benedek, T. (1938). Attention to reality in early infancy. *Psychoanalytic Quarterly, 7*, 200–214.

Benjamin, L. S. (1974). Structural analysis of social behavior. *Psychological Review, 81*(5), 392–425.

Beres, D. (1957). Communication in psychoanalysis and in the creative process: A parallel. *Journal of the American Psychoanalytic Association, 5*, 408–23.

Bergman, A. (1999). *Ours, yours, mine: Mutuality and the emergence of the separate self.* Northvale, N.J.: Jason Aronson.

Bergmann, M. S. (1984). The Legend of Narcissus. *American Imago, 41*(4), 389–411.

Berliner, B. (1940). Libido and reality in masochism. *Psychoanalytic Quarterly, 9,* 322.

Bernstein, I. (1988). A woman's fantasy of being unfinished. In H. P. Blum, Y. Kramer, A. K. Richards, and A. D. Richards (Eds.), *Fantasy, myth and reality: Essays in honor of Jacob A. Arlow, M.D.* (217–32). Madison, Conn.: International Universities Press.

Bion, W. R. (1983). *Attention and interpretation.* New York and London: Jason Aronson, Inc.

Black, H. C. (1990). *Black's law dictionary, sixth edition.* St. Paul, Minn.: West Publishing.

Blatt, S. J. (1974). Levels of object representation in anaclitic and introjective depression. *Psychoanalytic Study of the Child, 29,* 107–57.

Boesky, D. (1990). The psychoanalytic process and its components. *Psychoanalytic Quarterly, 59,* 550–84.

Bollas, C. (1987). *The shadow of the object: Psychoanalysis of the unthought known.* New York: Columbia University Press.

Boris, H. N. (1990). Identification with a vengeance. *International Journal of Psychoanalysis, 71,* 127–40.

Brenner, I. (1996). On trauma, perversion, and "multiple personality." *Journal of the American Psychoanalytic Association, 44,* 785–814.

Brice, C. W. (2000). Panel Report: Spontaneity versus constraint: Dilemmas in the analyst's decision making. *Journal of the American Psychoanalytic Association, 48,* 549–60.

Briggs, J. (1992) *Fractals: The patterns of chaos.* New York. Touchstone.

Bringing Up Baby. (1938). Movie produced and directed by H. Hawks; story by H. Wilde. RKO Radio Pictures.

Busch, F. (2007). "I noticed": The emergence of self-observation in relationship to pathological attractor sites. *International Journal of Psychoanalysis, 88,* 423–41.

Burland, J. A. (1996). Personal communication.

Caper, R. (1997). A mind of one's own. *International Journal of Psychoanalysis, 78,* 2265–78.

Casement, P. (1990). The meeting of needs in psychoanalysis. *Psychoanalytic Inquiry, 10,* 325–46.

Cernuschi, C., and Herczinski, A. (2007). Cutting Pollock down to size. In E. G. Landau and C. Cernuschi (Eds.), *Pollock matters* (73–90).

Cernuschi, C., Herczinski, A., and Martin, D. (2007). Abstract expressionism and fractal geometry. In E. G. Landau and C. Cernuschi (Eds.), *Pollock matters* (91–104).

Chused, J. F. (2001). Paper presented at Symposium 2001: What analysts do: Interpretation and beyond. New York, February 25.

Clark, M. (1988). *Jaques Lacan: An annotated bibliography*. New York and London: Garland Publishing.

Coates, S. (1998). Having a mind of one's own and holding the other in mind: Commentary on a paper by Peter Fonagy and Mary Target. *Psychoanalytic Dialogues, 8*, 115–48.

Coles, R. (1965). On courage. *Contemporary Psychoanalysis, 1*, 85–98.

Cooper, S. H. (2000). *Objects of hope: Exploring possibility and limit in psychoanalysis*. Hillsdale, N.J.: Analytic Press.

Dahl, H., and Teller, V. (1986). The microstructure of free association. *Journal of the American Psychoanalytic Association, 34*, 763–98.

Duez, B. (1996). L'effet Pygmalion: de l'originaire au transfert. *Cahiers Binet-Simon*, 647–48, 117–38.

Eidelson, R. J. (1997). Complex adaptive systems in the behavioral and social sciences. *Review of General Psychology, 1*(1), 42–71.

Emde, R. N. (1991). Positive emotions for psychoanalytic theory: Surprises from infancy research and new directions. *Journal of the American Psychoanalytic Association, 39*, 5–44.

Etezady, M. H. (1990). A summarized report of "Dandelion Children," a presentation by E. James Anthony. Association for Child Psychoanalysis and the Vulnerable Child Workshop, Santa Fe, New Mexico, April 6.

Fenichel, O. (1945). *The psychoanalytic theory of neurosis*. New York and London: Norton.

Fliess, R. (1942). The metapsychology of the analyst. *Psychoanalytic Quarterly, 11*, 221–27.

Fraiberg, S. (1969). Libidinal object constancy and mental representation. *Psychoanalytic Study of the Child, 24*, 9–47.

Frank, K. A. (1997). The role of the analyst's inadvertent self-revelations. *Psychoanalytic Dialogues*, 7, 281–314.

Freud, A. (1956). Comments on "A Mother's Observations." *Psychoanalytic Study of the Child, 11*, 427–33.

Freud, S. *The standard edition of the complete psychological works of Sigmund Freud*. Trans. J. Strachey. London: The Hogarth Press and the Institute of Psychoanalysis, 1964.

———. (1905). Three essays on sexuality. *Standard edition* 7.

———. (1905). Fragment of an analysis of a case of hysteria. *Standard edition* 7 (3–122).

———. (1912). Recommendations to physicians practising psychoanalysis. *Standard edition* 12 (111–20).

———. (1915). Observations on transference-love. *Standard edition* 12.

———. (1918). Recommendations to physicians practising psychoanalysis. *Standard edition* 12 (109–20).

———. (1919). A child is being beaten: A contribution to the study of the origin of sexual perversions. *Standard edition* 17.

———. (1919). The "uncanny." *Standard edition* 17 (219–56).

———. (1924). The economic problem of masochism. *Standard edition* 19.
———. (1933). New introductory lectures on psycho-analysis: Lecture XXXV. A weltanschauung? *Standard edition* 22 (158–82).
———. (1937). Analysis terminable and interminable. *Standard edition* 23 (209–53).
Frost, R. (1914). http://eir.library.utoronto.ca/rpo/display/poem847.html.
Gabbard, G. O. (1996). *Love and Hate in the Analytic Setting*. Northvale, N.J.: Jason Aronson, Inc.
Galatzer-Levy, R. M. (1995). Psychoanalysis and dynamical systems theory: Predictions and self-similarity. *Journal of the American Psychoanalytic Association, 43*, 1085–13.
Gay, P. (1989). *Freud: A Life for Our Time*. New York: Anchor Books.
Ghent, E. (1990). Masochism, submission, surrender—masochism as a perversion of surrender. *Contemporary Psychoanalysis, 26*, 108–36.
Giovacchini, P. L. (1957). Shaw's *Major Barbara*: A study of communication. Paper presented at the Annual Meeting of the American Psychoanalytic Association, Chicago.
Gladwell, M. (2005). *Blink*. New York and Boston: Little Brown and Company
Gleick, J. (1987). *Chaos: Making a new science*. New York. Penguin Books.
Glick, R. A. (2003). Idealization and psychoanalytic learning. *Psychoanalytic Quarterly, 72*, 377–401.
Goldstein, R. (2005). *Incompleteness: The proof and paradox of Kurt Gödel*. New York and London: W.W. Norton & Co.
Green, A. (1975). The analyst, symbolization and absence in the analytic setting (On changes in analytic practice and analytic experience). *International Journal of Psycho-Analysis, 56*(1), 1–22.
Greenberg, J. (1995). Self-disclosure: Is it psychoanalytic? *Contemporary Psychoanalysis, 31*, 193–205.
Grunes, M. (1984) The therapeutic object relationship. *Psychoanalytic Review, 71*(1), 123–43.
Guttman, S. A., Jones, R. L., and Parrish, S. M. (Eds.). (1980). *The concordance to the standard edition to the complete psychological works of Sigmund Freud*. Boston: G.K. Hall & Co.
Haley, C., Banks, W. C., and Zimbardo, P. (1973) Interpersonal dynamics in a simulated prison. *International Journal of Criminology & Penology, 1*, 69–97.
Hall, N. (Ed.). (1991). *Exploring chaos: A guide to the new science of disorder*. New York. W.W. Norton & Co.
Harris, A. (2005) *Gender as soft sssembly*. Hillsdale, N.J.: Analytic Press.
Hanly, C. (1998). Reflections on the analyst's self-disclosure. *Psychoanalytic Inquiry, 18*, 550–65.
Hoffer, A. (1985). Toward a definition of psychoanalytic neutrality. *Journal of the American Psychoanalytic Association, 33*, 771–95.
Hoffman, I. (1994) Dialectical thinking and therapeutic action in the psychoanalytic process. *Psychoanalytic Quarterly, 63*, 187–218.

Jacobs, T. (1999). On the question of self-disclosure by the analyst. *Psychoanalytic Quarterly, 68*, 159–83.

———. (1998). The one-person–two-person controversy: A view from the future. Paper presented at the Scientific Session of the Philadelphia Association for Psychoanalysis, January 9.

Kantrowitz, J. L. (1996). *The patient's impact on the analyst.* Hillsdale, N.J.: The Analytic Press.

Keats, J. (1819). Ode on a Grecian urn. http://www.bartleby.com/101/625, 2003.

Kernberg, O. (1976). *Object relations theory and clinical psychoanalysis.* New York: Jason Aronson.

———. (1992). *Aggression in personality disorders and perversions.* New Haven, Conn.: Yale Univ. Press.

Kohut, H. (1971). *The analysis of the self.* New York: International Universities Press.

———. (1977). *The restoration of the self.* New York: International Universities Press.

———. (1981). The psychoanalyst and the historian. In C. B. Strozier (Ed.), *Self psychology and the humanities.* New York and London: Norton, 1985.

———. (1985). On courage. In C. B. Strozier (Ed.), *Self psychology and the humanities.* New York and London: Norton.

Kris, E. (1956). On some vicissitudes of insight in psycho-analysis. *International Journal of Psychoanalysis, 37*, 445–55.

Lacan, J. (1936). The mirror stage as formative of the function of the I as revealed in psychoanalytic experience. In A. Sheridan (Trans.), *Ecrits, a selection.* New York: Norton, 1977.

———. (1958). The meaning of the phallus. In J. Mitchell and J. Rose (Eds.), *Feminine sexuality: Jacques Lacan and the ecole freudienne*, trans. J. Rose. New York: Norton.

———. (1977). *Ecrits: A Selection.* Trans. Alan Sheridan. New York: W.W. Norton & Company.

Lachmann, F. M., and Lichtenberg, J. (1992) Model scenes; implications for psychoanalytic treatment. *Journal of the American Psychoanalytic Association, 40*, 117–37.

Landau, E. G., and Cernuschi, C. (Eds.). (2007). *Pollock matters.* Boston and Chicago: McMullan Museum of Art, Boston College, and the University of Chicago Press.

Lear, J. (1998). *Love and its place in nature: A philosophical interpretation of Freudian psychoanalysis.* New Haven, Conn., and London: Yale University Press.

———. (2002). Jumping from the couch: An essay on phantasy and emotional structure. *International Journal of Psychoanalysis, 83*, 583–95.

Lee, J. S. (1990). *Jacques Lacan.* Amherst: University of Massachusetts Press.

Levenson, E. A. (1983). *The ambiguity of change: An inquiry into the nature of psychoanalytic reality.* New York: Basic Books.

———. (1994). The uses of disorder: chaos theory and psychoanalysis. *Contemporary Psychoanalysis, 30*, 5–24.

———. (1996). Aspects of self-revelation and self-disclosure. *Contemporary Psychoanalysis, 32*, 237–248.

Levine, S. S. (1996). *Useful servants: Psychodynamic approaches to clinical practice.* Northvale, N.J.: Jason Aronson.

———. (1997). Paying and reality: Discussion of Edward R. Shapiro's "The boundaries are shifting: renegotiating the therapeutic frame." Paper presented at the Scientific Session of the Philadelphia Psychoanalytic Society, October 15.

———. (2001). On the mirror stage with Henry and Eliza, or playing with *Pygmalion* in five acts. *Journal of Applied Psychoanalytic Studies, 3*(2), 103–25.

———. (2001b). Review of Lear's *Love and its place in nature: A philosophical interpretation of Freudian psychoanalysis. Journal of Applied Psychoanalytic Studies, 3*(3), 289–92.

———. (2003). Beauty treatment: The aesthetics of the psychoanalytic process. *Psychoanalytic Quarterly, 72*, 987–1016.

———. (2004). To have and to hold: On the experience of having an Other. *Psychoanalytic Quarterly, 73*, 934–69.

———. (2006). Catching the wrong leopard: Courage and masochism in the psychoanalytic situation. *Psychoanalytic Quarterly, 75*, 533–56.

———. (2007). Nothing but the truth: Self-disclosure, self-revelation, and the persona of the analyst. *Journal of the American Psychoanalytic Association* 55, 1.

Levy, S. T. (2005). The natural. Paper presented at the Psychoanalytic Center of Philadelphia, May 24.

Levy, S. T., and Inderbitzen, L. B. (1992). Neutrality, interpretation, and therapeutic intent. *Journal of the American Psychoanalytic Association, 40*, 989–1011.

Likierman, M. (1989). Clinical significance of aesthetic experience. *International Review of Psychoanalysis, 16*, 133–50.

Loewald, H. W. (1960). On the therapeutic action of psycho-analysis. *International Journal of Psycho-Analysis, 41*(1), 16–33.

———. (1975). Psychoanalysis as art and the fantasy character of the psychoanalytic situation. *Journal of the American Psychoanalytic Association, 23*, 277–99.

Loewenstein, R. (1957). A contribution to the psychoanalytic theory of masochism. *Journal of the American Psychoanalytic Association, 5*, 197–234.

Lorenz, E. (1979) Predictability: Does the flap of a butterfly's wings in Brazil set off a tornado in Texas? Address, annual meeting of the American Association for the Advancement of Science, cited in Gleick (1987).

Luborsky, L., and Crits-Christoph, P. (1990). *Understanding transference: The core conflictual relationship theme method.* New York: Basic Books.

Mahony, P. J. (1996). *Freud's Dora: A psychoanalytic, historical, and textual study.* New Haven, Conn., and London: Yale University Press.

Maleson, F. G. (1984). The multiple meanings of masochism in psychoanalytic discourse. *Journal of the American Psychoanalytic Association, 32*, 325–56.

Margulies, A. (1993). Contemplating the mirror of the other; empathy and self-analysis. In J. Barron (Ed.), *Self-analysis: Critical inquiries, personal visions*. Hillsdale, N.J.: The Analytic Press.

Meissner, W. W. (2002). The problem of self-disclosure in psychoanalysis. *Journal of the American Psychoanalytic Association, 50*, 827–67.

Meyer, B. C. (1984). Some observations on the rescue of fallen women. *Psychoanalytic Quarterly, 53*(2), 208–39.

Milgram, S. (1974). *Obedience to authority*. New York: Harper & Row.

Miller, J. H. (1990). *Versions of Pygmalion*. Cambridge, Mass.: Harvard University Press.

Mitchell, S. A. (1998). The analyst's knowledge and authority. *Psychoanalytic Quarterly, 67*(1), 1–31.

Mitrani, J. L. (1998). Unbearable ecstasy, reverence and awe, and the perpetuation of an "aesthetic conflict." *Psychoanalytic Quarterly, 67*(1), 102–27.

Moore, B. E., and Fine, B. D. (1990). *Psychoanalytic terms and concepts*. New Haven, Conn., and London: American Psychoanalytic Association and Yale University Press.

Moran, M. G. (1991). Chaos theory and psychoanalysis: The fluidic nature of the mind. *International Journal of Psychoanalysis, 18*, 211–21.

Novey, S. (1958). The meaning of the concept of mental representation of objects. *Psychoanalytic Quarterly, 27*, 57–79.

Novick, J., and Novick, K. K. (1987). The essence of masochism. *Psychoanalytic Study of the Child, 42*, 353–84.

Olsson, P. (1994). A psychoanalytic study of integrity, inner courage, and "good character." *Mind & Human Interaction, 5*(1), 34–41.

The Oxford English dictionary. (2005). http://dictionary.oed.com/cgi/entry _main/00052295?query_type=word&queryword=courage&edition=2e&first=1&max_to_show=10&sort_type=alpha.

Ogden, T. (1994). The analytical third: Working with intersubjective clinical facts. *International Journal of Psychoanalysis, 75*, 3–20.

———. (2005). On psychoanalytic writing. *International Journal of Psychoanalysis, 86*, 15–29.

Ovid. (1). *Metamorphoses*. http://en.wikisource.org/wiki/Metamorphoses/Book_X.

Parens, H. (1970). Inner sustainment: Metapsychological considerations. *Psychoanalytic Quarterly, 39*, 223–39.

———. (1979). *The development of aggression in early childhood*. New York: Jason Aronson.

———. (2003). Personal communication.

Pfeffer, A. (1961). Follow-up study of a satisfactory analysis. *Journal of the American Psychoanalytic Association, 9*, 698–718.

Poland, W. (1998). Personal communication.

Prince, R. (1974). Courage and masochism in psychotherapy. *Psychoanalytic Review, 71*(1), 47–61.

Procci, W. (2002). Panel report: Chaos theory as a new paradigm in psychoanalysis: A contribution to the discussion of models. *International Journal of Psychoanalysis, 83*, 1–4.

Psychoanalytic Electronic Publishing CD-ROM Conference. (1999). Analytic hours: The good, the bad, and the ugly. New York, February.

Pygmalion. (1938). Movie directed by Anthony Asquith and Leslie Howard. Screenplay by George Bernard Shaw. Criterion Collection.

Quinodoz, J.-M. (1997). Transitions in psychic structures in the light of deterministic chaos theory. *International Journal of Psychoanalysis, 78*, 699–718.

Rachman, S. (1984). Fear and courage. *Behavior Therapy, 15*, 109–20.

Raphling, D. L. (1992). Some vicissitudes of aggression in the interpretive process. *Psychoanalytic Quarterly, 61*, 352–69.

———. (1995). Interpretation and expectation: The anxiety of influence. *Journal of the American Psychoanalytic Association, 43*, 95–111.

Reid, J. D. (1993). *The Oxford guide to classical mythology in the arts, 1300–1990s.* New York and Oxford: Oxford University Press.

Renik, O. (1993). Analytic interaction: Conceptualizing technique in light of the analyst's irreducible subjectivity. *Psychoanalytic Quarterly, 62*, 553–71.

———. (1995). The ideal of the anonymous analyst and the problem of self-disclosure. *Psychoanalytic Quarterly, 64*, 466–95.

———. (1999). Playing one's cards face up in analysis: An approach to the problem of self-disclosure. *Psychoanalytic Quarterly, 68*, 521–39.

Richardson, H. B. (1956). The Pygmalion reaction. *The Psychoanalytic Review, 43*, 458–60.

Rose, G. (1980). *The power of form.* New York: International Universities Press.

Rose, J. (1985). Introduction-II. In J. Mitchell and J. Rose (Eds.), *Feminine sexuality: Jacques Lacan and the ecole freudienne*, trans. J. Rose (22–57). New York: Norton.

Rothstein, A. (1995). A perspective on analysts' evaluating, diagnosing, and prognosticating. Paper presented at Philadelphia Psychoanalytic Society, September.

Sander, L. W. (1983). Polarity, paradox, and the organizing process in development. In J. Call, R. E. Galenson, and R. L. Tyson (Eds.), *Frontiers of infant psychiatry* (333–46). New York: Basic Books

Saul, L., and Warner, S. (1967). Identity and a point of technique. *Psychoanalytic Quarterly, 36*, 532–45.

Schafer, R. (1968). *Aspects of internalization.* New York: International Universities Press.

———. (1983). *The analytic attitude.* New York: Basic Books.

Segal, H. (1952). A psycho-analytic approach to aesthetics. In R. Frankiel (Ed.), *Essential papers on object loss* (486–507). New York: New York University Press, 1994.

Shaw, G. B. (1941). *Pygmalion.* New York: Penguin Books.

Silvio, J. R. (1995). George Bernard Shaw's *Pygmalion*: A creative response to early childhood loss. *Journal of the American Academy of Psychoanalysis, 23*(2), 234–334.

Sharpless, E. (1985). Identity formation as reflected in the acquisition of person pronouns. *Journal of the American Psychoanalytic Association, 330*, 861–85.

Shengold, L. (1991). *Soul murder: The effects of childhood abuse and deprivation*. New York: Ballantine Books.

Skolnick, N. J., and Scharff, D. E. (Eds.). (1998). *Fairbairn, then and now*. Hillsdale, N.J.: Analytic Press.

Smith, H. F. (1993). Engagements in the analytic work. *Psychoanalytic Inquiry, 13*, 425–54.

———. (1995). Analytic listening and the experience of surprise. *International Journal of Psychoanalysis, 76*, 67–78.

———. (2000). Countertransference, conflictual listening, and the analytic object relationship. *Journal of the American Psychoanalytic Association, 48*, 95–128.

Spitz, R. (1965). *The first year of life: A psychoanalytic study of normal and deviant development of object relations*. New York: International Universities Press.

Spruiell, V. (1993). Deterministic chaos theory and the sciences of complexity: Psychoanalysis in the midst of a general scientific revolution. *Journal of the American Psychoanalytic Association, 41*, 3–44.

Stein, M. H. (1966). Self observation, reality, and the superego. In R. Loewenstein, L. Newman, M. Schur and A. Solnit (Eds.), *Psychoanalysis—A general psychology: Essays in honor of Heinz Hartmann* (275–97). New York: International Universities Press.

Stern, Daniel. (1985). *The interpersonal world of the infant: A view from psychoanalysis and developmental psychology*. New York: Basic Books.

Stern, Donnel. (1999). Psychoanalytic interaction and the intuition of freedom. Paper presented at "Analytic Hours: The Good, the Bad, and the Ugly," Psychoanalytic Electronic Publishing CD-ROM Conference, New York, February.

Strenger, C. (1989). The classic and the romantic vision in psychoanalysis. *International Journal of Psychoanalysis, 70*, 593–610.

Talpin, J-M. (1997). Narcisse et Pygmalion: Le décollement esthétique. *Adolescence, 15*(1), 175–85.

Taylor, R. P. (2002). Order in Pollock's chaos. *Scientific American*, December, 116–21.

Vesonder, T. G. (1977). Eliza's choice: Transformation myth and the ending of Pygmalion. In R. Weintraub (Ed.), *Fabian feminist: Bernard Shaw and women* (39–45). University Park and London: Pennsylvania State University Press.

Weissman, P. (1958). Shaw's childhood and *Pygmalion*. *Psychoanalytic Study of the Child, 13*, 541–61.

Winnicott, D. W. (1951). *Playing and Reality*. Middlesex, UK: Penguin Books.

———. (1960). *The maturational processes and the facilitating environment*. New York: International Universities Press.

———. (1963). Psychotherapy of character disorders. In *The maturational processes and the facilitating environment* (203–16). New York: International Universities Press, 1965.

———. (1971). *Playing and reality*. New York: Penguin Books.

Zeman, A. (2002) *Consciousness: A user's guide*. New Haven, Conn., and London. Basic Books.

Index

About the Author

Susan S. Levine, L.C.S.W., B.C.D., is in the private practice of psychoanalysis, psychotherapy, and clinical supervision in Ardmore, Pennsylvania, and is on the faculty of the Institute of the Psychoanalytic Center of Philadelphia and of the Center for Psychoanalysis in the Department of Psychiatry at Albert Einstein Medical Center. She earned her graduate degree in clinical social work at the Bryn Mawr College Graduate School of Social Work and Social Research in 1982, studied psychoanalytic psychotherapy at the Philadelphia Psychoanalytic Institute, and completed psychoanalytic training at the Institute of the Psychoanalytic Center of Philadelphia in 2002. She has been a faculty member in the graduate programs in social work at Bryn Mawr College and at Widener University. A former editorial associate at the *International Journal of Psychoanalysis*, she is currently on the editorial board of the *Clinical Social Work Journal*. Her first book was *Useful Servants: Psychodynamic Approaches to Clinical Practice* (1996).

www.ingramcontent.com/pod-product-compliance
Ingram Content Group UK Ltd.
Pitfield, Milton Keynes, MK11 3LW, UK
UKHW012041150926
475560UK00001B/133

9 780765 706249